OUTRAGEOUS

REALITY

By Eddy Hill

DEDICATION

THIS BOOK IS DEDICATED TO ALL MY FRIENDS AND FAMILY WHO HELPED
TO MAKE THESE STORES TRUE.

EDDY HILL

CKNOWLEDGMENTS

To my wife Cozy.

EDDY HILL

CONTENTS

PREFACE

START READING THIS BOOK HERE

This is a friendly shot at writing a few pages about all the wisdom available to an old f--- geezer approaching 90.

"How come we get so soon old and so late smart?"

The first time you heard that you thought it applied only to the ancient ones.

At the age of 50 you feel that you have picked up a little wisdom.

At 60 you begin to wonder why you are wasting your time in the rat race.

At 70 you begin to see the past clearly and the future becomes a bonus.

At 80 you gain serenity from the respect you get just for having beaten the odds against living this long. If you could turn back the clock, you'd be happy just to be a sexagenarian again, no pun intended.

Here's an enigma: If you could turn back the calendar, you could take some of the money you now have [and don't need] and give it to yourself at a younger age, when, if you had had it, would probably have shortened your life with it.

This book is half serious and half fun…as your life should be.

CHAPTER 1 - HOW TO STOP SUICIDE BOMBING

We should announce to the Palestinians, the Iraqis, and any other Islamic eager to get into heaven that from now on all such bombers dead bodies or body parts will be wrapped in PIG SKINS before burial. According to their folklore this would send their souls to hell or whatever nether regions they wished to avoid.

We had a similar problem during and after the Spanish-American War in the Philippine Islands where a lot of the "insurgents" were of the Muslim persuasion. Our Marines found that these jungle fighters totally lost their cool when threatened with a pigskin coat. They would give up their firstborn rather than become part of a ham sandwich.

THE OCCULT WILL WIN US OVER

Baal, Apollo, Allah, God, et al, has provided us fearful humans with HOPE and will continue to do so as long as we seek their favor. We all have an occult spot in the brain that is hungry for the comfort for Gods. There is always the unpopular possibility that when we each die we will be extinct. The HORROR of that chance is why atheists are always in the minority.

An old geezer once said: "The truth is just a lie that folks like to live with."

SAINTS 21, COWBOYS 7, RAMS 0

The Vatican likes to make saints out of "do-gooders," but they have to wait until they are dead. The kinds of names of people made into saints change over the centuries in accordance with the general population's taste for such names. Today we don't see many kids in our schools named Stanislaus, Sverdrif, Elmo or even Steffen, but a hundred years from now new saints will bear such names as Bubba, Billy Bob, etc. There might even be a Saint Debbie. Heaven forbid.

ENVIRONS

We probably couldn't affect the environment if we tried. If the earth is getting any warmer, nobody knows why. According to Michael Crichton's exhaustive study of scientific research papers, there is little to worry about in carbon monoxide changes or sea level variations.

If we should ever have global warming, it will increase the crop yields. Environmentalists seem to be exploiting the environment. Every so often new sources of energy seem to come along. Remember, in 1800 we had only human and horse muscles to work for us.

Anyone who is "certain" is crazy, I'm certain of that.

No one blames themselves.

The greedy are also incompetent and the incompetent are also greedy.

Some people say that when they had a dictator things ran better.

Half the world lives on $2.00 a day.

People are more likely to believe a politician than a scientist. The Pols want to keep us scared. "There will be a terrible depression. The Nazis will invade us. The Yellow Peril is coming. The Commies will bomb us. Asbestos will kill you. Tap water is poison. Power lines cause cancer. Killer bees are on their way. West Nile, Mad Cow, Bird Flu, Terrorists, Weapons of Mass Destruction, Iran, North Korea, Libya, etc, etc."

What about giant corporations, the mass media and the "un-American" people against wars of aggression, and inefficient companies that would go broke without illegal labor?

I understand there are petitions going around to ban DIHYDROGEN MONOXYGEN. It's in our lakes and rivers and in all our fruits and veggies. Watch out for it. The chemical formula is H2O.

Some dogs are sexists. A feminist was chased by a Doberperson.

In some areas, if you are not loud you are a wimp.

The loudest people are Red, White and Blue.

White trash

Red neck

Blue collar

If you gave a minority his choice of skin color, would that make him want to work hard and succeed?

Harpo is Oprah spelled backwards, but they have little in common.

CHAPTER 2 - BALLOT MEASURES

During the national elections, which happen every two years, the voters of many states tack on a proposition or two to settle a dispute or to pass a law that the state or local law makers are loath to legislate because the "deep pocket people" are passing out piles of re-election money (bribes) with strong strings attached.

The "sitting" politicians properly predict that the people will not provide funds for their next campaign. Therefore, we always end up with "Legislation by Lobbyists." And, our boys in the state capitals are usually happy to have the lobbyists actually write the laws that affect us all.

But when the People get together to write an Initiative or Referendum or Proposition, the special interests are usually out of the picture and they have to spend millions to try to defeat the measure. If it works so well at the state level, why not try it at the national level? They do it a lot in Switzerland, New Zealand, and other countries, so why not here. You say the U.S. is too big? That just means we have more people to collect the signatures.

There are some simple laws that the majority wants but which our Congress could never pass. The lobbyists won't allow it. They get too rich and powerful by keeping such good things off the books. And how can you expect our greedy governors to pass anything against their own interests?

Here are just a few of the things the majority of us WANT:

Gun and ammo registration.

Election finance reform.

Term limits.

Price control on prescription drugs.

Bank interest rates control.

Nuisance law suits outlawed.

Loser pays in law suits.

Religion scams revealed and punished.

Welfare scams investigated.

Electoral College abolishment.

Corporate Official's pay scandals.

Discrimination in religion, race or sexual orientation.

Illegal alien control.

Border control.

Alien work programs instituted.

National identity and citizenship records.

Terrorist attack readiness.

Tourist and student visa follow-up.

Out-sourcing control.

Science educational promotions.

Social Security funds protection from Congress.

Federal pay cuts during deficits.

High Federal fines for dope USERS.

Cancellation of tobacco subsidies.

Auto pollution reduction.

Atomic Energy incentives.

Prison reform.

Family planning incentives.

Tax reform.

National forest conservation.

Clean water enforcement.

Imported cargo inspection.

Health insurance similar to those successful plans used in other countries.

Cell-phone-free areas in restaurants and airlines.

Most of the above are self explanatory; some will be further discussed later.

Some will say that our country is too big to have our citizens vote on such matters. Isn't that why they invented the Electoral College, we were just too big to vote for a president?

Politicians are like diapers. They should be changed often, and for the same reason.

CHAPTER 3 – HIGH TAILING IT INTO TOWN

At the edge of town a proud and perfect tumble weed was completing its parade down Main Street. It would now exit into the oblivion of the desert. Then the afternoon shadows preceded a rugged old prospector riding a tall mule and leading a shorter burro piled high with gear. The trio went straight to the state assay office of Carson City where his small pouch of yellow dust brought him ninety dollars in paper money. A 90 day trek was over yet he visited the town as seldom as necessary. It was better out there.

The next stop was the livery stable where the animals were given oats and water. The sweaty animals smacked their lips at this rare treat. When the feast was finished the three filed further a field until they reached a saloon which sported an old sign that read, "The Cork Café," probably a tribute to its Irish heritage.

Pete the prospector tied up Lilly the tall mule and Umberto the standard burro to the hitching rail. His previous owner had referred to him as "Un Burro," thus the classy cognomen. Pete walked up the two wooden steps and pushed through the swinging doors that groaned to announce his arrival.

The place was awash with the loud playing of the blind black piano player and the shouts of the rowdy revelers. Miss Kitty was busy fending off her offender, Jake McGillicuddy, the hard-ass son of the local land baron. Every one in town felt that they had to tolerate the tin horn tyrant so they laughed long and loud with him, but they laughed at him behind his back. Miss Kitty was a bit scruffy but unpretentious.

As the dirty old man walked slowly up to the bar, all eyes were following him. He leaned his old rusty trusty rifle up against the bar and faced the barkeep who cocked his head and asked, "Well if it ain't Pete, you here for your quarter-annual beer and whisky shot?" Pete said nary a word as he placed a dime and a nickel on the bar and waited patiently for the "elixir of life" to arrive.

Jake stopped groping Kitty and shouted, "You old fart, you're stinking up the hall!" Pete took a dainty preliminary sip of the rye in the small glass and let it soak into his parched tongue. Then he sampled the beer in the mug. His eyes glinted as he seemed to shrink lower into his clothes. "I'm talking to you, you dirty old man," Jake continued. "How would you like to do a little dance for us?" He pulled out his two shiny pistols and fired two shots into the sandy floor near Pete's grubby boots.

The explosion of the two 45 caliber shots caught Pete's attention so he turned to face his tormentor. As more shots started he began to jump and dance to keep the bullets from hitting his feet. Higher and higher he jumped as the explosions and gun smoke filled the hall. Suddenly all was quiet—except for the clicking of the pistol hammers as they rammed against the now expired tiny detonators of the empty shell casings.

The crowd was still in awe as Jake started emptying one of the revolver's cylinders to reload. He was so busy he did not notice the crowd shifting their attention to Pete who was calmly lifting his rifle. He raised the heavy barrel and pointed it at Jake. As he pulled the hammer back, the double click could be heard in the farthest corner of the hall.

The scion looked up, blanched, and stuttered, "Wait a minute, sir, I didn't…now hold it, I was jest funnin'. Put that barrel down, please, sir."

In the tomb-like silence that followed, Pete finally spoke. He drawled, "Did you ever kiss a mule's ass?"

The explosion of laughter could be heard all the way to the edge of town where a new perfect tumble weed was preparing to taxi out for its parade down Main Street. The evening breeze urged it forward onto its final journey.

CHAPTER 4 - THE NICENE CREED

This was a religious belief statement written in the olden town of Nicaea. In 325 A.D. a council was convened there to settle some serious disagreements as whether Jesus had been a man, God, or in between. Some maintained that he was of equal substance to God the Father, while others believed that He was a step below Godhood. The advocates for equal status won out and then the council decided to make the historic record, what little there was, conform to the new fact. They studied all the writings available on the subject and either approved or disapproved of them. The ones okayed were made official and put together as a New Testament. The rejected ones were now called The Apocrypha, many of which described Jesus' early life before the age of thirty.

One of these unaccepted stories described Jesus' visit to a certain village where the people doubted his legitimacy. Jesus resented this and struck the whole village blind. One can understand the Council's dissatisfaction with this story.

The main accepted stories often disagreed with each other in many respects, but regardless of this they were now the Words of God.

Linguists who study the word-flow of writers note that whenever direct quotes of Jesus' words are given, they seem to be written by a different author, especially whenever He says something about being a God.

Many Biblical scholars do not believe He ever claimed to be a real God. Of course, many famous Biblical scholars do not believe that there ever were any real miracles either. The debate goes on and keeps them all employed.

OTHER CREEDS

Polytheism: The belief that all religions are good.

Henotheism: I'll believe in yours if you believe in mine.

STUPID CAVE MEN

Caveman to woman: "Let me get this straight. You and I do this 'marriage' thing and then I can have all the sex I want with you but no one else, and if you ever get mad at me you will take the kids and the cave and you kick me out. Is that it?"

Woman: "That's right."

Caveman: "I'll buy that."

CHAPTER 5 - THINGS THAT SUCK

Soda straws

Leeches

Vacuum cleaners

Dark holes

Puppies

Kittens

Calves

Colts

Lambs

Fawns

Fellaton

Phone solicitations

CREATIVE WRITING

Some words defeat themselves. Like "pre-boarding." This means you get on the airplane before you get on. And "supernatural." This means it is more than natural? A lot of things are truly amazing, but still natural.

It took nature, here on earth, three billion years just to produce a Jellyfish.

It took another 500,000,000 years to produce a land animal..

About 5 million years ago, our ancestors started standing erect. Yippee.

It took a million years to go from grunts to words.

Then another million to go from words to sentences. This stuff is hard.

Then sentences went into questions which are still ongoing.

Some day, something magic may happen, but it will all be natural like everything else: most explainable, some, not yet. As for the SUPERNATURAL, so far, nothing.

A RITE

Marriage is a triumph of imagination over intelligence.

If a rock band has neither talent nor training, they must play really loud. I heard that once Sinatra had a drummer who got so loud he drowned out the sound of Frank. He fired him.

Bush, to waitress in coffee shop: "I'll have a quickie."

The waitress slapped him and left.

A second waitress, older, came up and said: "It's pronounced "Quiche"."

Country boy in a big city bar: "Hi ya, my name's Elmer, what's yours?"

"Fuck off, Bozo."

"Can I buy you a drink, Miss Bozo?"

There was an ancient rite in ancient times where they threw a virgin into a volcano to appease the Gods. Why a virgin? Because no one wanted to get rid of a bad girl!

LONELY GOAT HERDERS

In Asia, lonely goat herders used to amuse themselves by playing a stringed instrument called the SITAR. Little boys who would tend the baby goats played a smaller thing called the Baby Sitar. It was only used while looking after little kids.

COWBOY PHILOSOPHY

If women didn't have such a unique physiognomy, there'd be a bounty on 'em.

BIG GIRL

She was a very big girl. In a bikini she reminded you of a dead heat in a blimp race.

CHAPTER 6 - WHAT IF THERE WERE NO HYPOTHETICALS?

Old writers used to use the term "God-Speed." What does it mean? I'll tell you later, but first:

Part I:

What if we had a giant flash bulb whose diameter was as large as the distance from here to the sun? Now let's set it off and make a one second light burst that will be seen all over the universe. The light would shoot out in all directions at once [at the speed of light] and it could be seen at our nearest neighboring star, Alpha Centaurus, in about 4.2 years.

Light may travel 186,000 miles a second but its brightness dims as the square of the distance. In other words, after two years, it will be only one fourth as strong as it was after one year. Simple? Our light would travel outward for hundreds of years, thousands, millions. Some day, if there were an astronomer on the edge of the visible universe, he could see our one second flash if his equipment was good enough. Our faint light would still be going at 186,000 miles per second after, maybe 14 billion years [plus or minus 50%].

Part II:

The first was a conjecture from facts. Now let us surmise from theory.

In maybe half that time and distance, our light would have passed by Heaven which is at the center of the Universe. If we lead a good life, and if Jesus was right, we will get to go there after we pass on. There we will be joined with our ex-spouses, and their ex-spouses, parents, grandparents, ancestors, dogs, cats, horses and all previous neighbors to mingle and be happy for ever and ever. I think it will only take you about a day at "God's Speed" to get there as our souls have no substance or mass, so we are not limited as light is. Light has substance.

If light can go 570 million miles per hour, we would be traveling 290 million light years per hour. We won't see much scenery along the way, all a blur. And, yes, Virginia, when you ask God to help you find your kitty, it could take a day for your prayer to get there, and after processing and approval, it could take a day for help to arrive.

There must also be souls who go to Hell. These are the people who are infidels, atheists, Hindus, Taoists, Confucians, Muslims, certain Jews, All heathens, heretics, pagans, Buddhists, Jaiines, Incans, Aztecs, Native Americans, Eskimos, and many others.

We all know that when a tiny female egg is fertilized, an Angel puts in a little soul at that very instant. Sadly, three fourths of those little human beings die in the first ten days of natural causes so their souls go to heaven, unless they are recycled. If they are not reincarnated, then Heaven gets three fourths of its residents from this jolly embryonic group. One cell per each.

Some women would be excluded from Heaven because when an egg presents itself, if they do not fertilize it they ABORT it [according to Biologists]. Is Heaven only for men? But men cannot get in if they have had lustful thoughts. Oh, well, what the hell...

But there might be lots of members from other planets, if their planet ever discovered the blessings of religions. If every star has at least one planet, and if one planet in a MILLION has thinking life on it [ahead or behind us in evolution] then all those planets could send their souls to Heaven. NOTE: The number of peopled planets would be about 9,000,000,000,000,000. Fifteen zeros, more or less.

Note: This was calculated as follows; 300 billion stars in the Milky Way Galaxy - times - 30 billion other galaxies. That's a 9 followed by 21 zeros. And by our supposition only one star in a million has smart life on it, just take away 6 zeros and thus you are left with the 15 zeros mentioned above.

If conditions in Hell were too hot and crowded, souls could either extinguish themselves, or apply for reincarnation.

A little girl was asked about reincarnation. She said that it was when you laughed so hard at the dinner table that the milk came back out of your nose.

Answers can evince more questions. And people who think they know all the answers irk those who really do.

Don't you feel more like you do now ???

WHAT IF

What if they invented birth control for gays and lesbians?

Sulfa-denial Noacetol.

WHAT IF

What if a group of interplanetary powers arrived here and told us that from now on we would be required to use their idea of the perfect government? They would decree that in our national, state, and city governments, the "executive" branches must be headed up by a group of three elected officials. A Trioca? One would be the most intelligent person available, one would be the most experienced person in governmental affairs, and the third would be the person with the best leadership qualities.

 Are these the qualities we should use? Would the system work? Write YOUR congressman, MINE doesn't read mail.

CHAPTER 7 - THE ULTIMATE AIRLINE PLANE

Some day some Aeronautical Engineers will have to design an airline transport plane that meets the needs and can handle the restrictions of our finite airports. The number of new gates we can build is limited by many factors. In 1975, the late Art Ford, V.P. Planning at Delta Air Lines, said that in the next forty years (circa 2015) all the major air traffic hubs would be swamped to saturation and should be complimented by at least one new airport near each major hub. However, experience shows that local planning groups seldom look at the long range picture, so it appears we will suffer more and more congestion in our air traffic, ad in-flight finitum.

A larger plane, maybe a thousand seats, could be designed so as to not be dependant on a gate, whenever none is available. If the seating were arranged in say eight 125 seat independent compartments (gondolas?) these light weight units could be towed or driven off the aircraft right into the terminal building. There the passengers could debark at their leisure, out of the weather.

Such a plane would have a take-off gross weight of about 1,350,000 lbs and a range of 10,000 miles.

Before such a new aircraft can be type certificated and awarded an Airworthiness Placard, there must be a demonstration to prove that a full compliment of passengers can deplane in two minutes or less. This must be done with real people.

A military aircraft such as the C-5A can carry six Greyhound busses which it can load and unload through large doors at the nose and tail, with built-in ramps. The aforementioned eight gondolas could be unloaded in a hurry and thus satisfy this requirement for emergencies.

The Airbus A 380 will carry 800 passengers divided between two decks. In an emergency it will be a very long slide down a very flexible chute that is only supported by columns of air. In our compartmentalized design, each unit would carry its own luggage while the main airframe would have a cargo area below decks of a huge capacity.

Each unit would have its own drinking water and toilet, while the main airframe would supply the pressurization, heat, and air conditioning. Box lunches and beverages could be sold in the terminal waiting area and passengers would be asked to keep the used containers until debarkation, thus the cabin crew could be limited to one per unit.

An aircraft of this size would have space below decks for lots of cargo which is always good for revenue. That brings up the availability of a lot of space above the main deck. This could profitably be made into a sort of "club space" where anyone in coach or other class could ascend to this upper level and stretch out, buy a drink, snack, or sandwich and maybe just look out the windows at the scenery. There would not be room for everyone at the same time so a charge of, say, one hundred dollars for this blissful place seems fair. Of course it could not be occupied during takeoff or landing and seat belts would have to be provided for rough weather and turbulence.

Some day this type of air transport will have to be built unless a way is found to eliminate airports entirely. The crystal ball says that is not likely in our lifetimes.

CHAPTER 8 - ANTEDELUVIAN

It hadn't rained for many fortnights. Grandpa's leg said it should rain. This was about 6000 years before calendars (b.c.). The wild onions and other unnamed roots needed rain. The drought reigned even to the plains in Spain.

A man was called The Woodcutter because he was always making things out of wood. He had a household near the Tigris River long before rivers had names; even the Euphrates had no name.

Grandpa said, "When it doesn't rain the rain piles up into a big pond in the sky, and the longer it takes, the bigger grows the pond. There must be a lake of water up there by now and when it spills out it's gonna swamp everything. Son, you better get ready to tie the wife and kids to some trees, or comes the deluge, they'll all be goners. In all my born days yada yada yada — my bum leg says its gonna really rain."

The eldest boy, One Son, had been cutting down trees to make more farmland and also to impress the neighbor girls. When he had a lot of logs laying around he decided to make them into a big raft. The neighbor girls, Dizzy, Mitzy, and Ditzy, made fun of him. Dizzy said, "Hey, Monkey Man, how you ever gonna get such a big raft down to the river?" One Son ignored her. Ditzy said, "Maybe you kin git one of your numb nuts brothers to carry it fer ya."

Mitzy just gave him the finger. She had six on each hand. One Son went and got two of his brothers, Two Son and Fee Nix to help him, and soon the raft got really huge. It got to be a stone's throw long. Their old mother nagged, "Stop playing with your logs. You kids should be out digging wild onions and stuff, have you forgotten yer roots?" Then it started to sprinkle a bit.

The Woodcutter looked at their raft and said, "If'n it pours like grandpa's leg says it will, we're might gonna need this here raft. Maybe you could put some hand rails along the edges so's nobody gits inundated overboard." One Son was proud. "I named it 'The Bark'." Then he asked, "Pa, do ya think we should make one end kinda pointy?" The Woodcutter replied, "Why? It ain't goin no wheres."

Soon the pond spilled out of the sky and Grandpa said, "It's raining like a cow pissin on a flat rock." For four days and four nights it rained hard. The river rose, the fields flooded, and the woods were awash. The flood covered the whole world, as they knew it. The old mother warned, "We will be washed away! Noah (her special nickname for her husband), Do something, I'm drenched, we'll be drowned."

The Woodcutter called for a clan meeting. "Gather up some of the goats, a pair of horses, a couple of cows, the coop of chickens and the herd of hogs, and corral them all on the Bark. This might be a flood of biblical proportions. Hurry!" After furious hours of work, they and their livestock were huddled in the hard rain, adrift on the raft. The Woodcutter began to make a hut on the raft for shelter.

The three sons were surprised and intrigued by the sight of the three neighbor girls floundering in the flotsam and ululating to get their attention. Dizzy bellowed, "Ahoy, Brainy Boys, bring us on board." Ditzy screamed, "We shall be beholden beyond belief." Mitzy added, "Even fellatio!"

Needless to say, the girls were taken up on the raft and by the time the waters receded the three brothers had married the three sisters (all slightly pregnant) in a ceremony presided over by their father, the Head-of-the-Ship. They surveyed their new surroundings and it was good. The Woodcutter announced, "We have come a long ways down the river. Now let us demarcate these fields as our own." The old mother nagged, "Noah, if'n you'd made a bigger raft, I coulda brought more of my stuff, like my other dress."

The story of the voyage of the Bark was repeated down through all the generations of the Middle East. Tribal story tellers could seldom resist the temptation to embellish the beloved story called "The Woodcutter's Family and their Raft, the Bark."

Eventually, over time, it was just called "Noak's Bark."

CHAPTER 9 - SLOW SUICIDE

If you insure yourself for a zillion bucks and then commit suicide, the payoff will be denied. One guy decided he had found a loop hole. He would get the BIG policy and then ride an airline every day until he crashed. Good idea, except it would take a while. Like 21,000 years.

Until you see the statistics it's hard to realize how many planes full of people are in the air at any one minute. We probably read about an airline crash about once a year and it's usually a big mystery as to why it happened. By the time the accident investigation is completed, maybe a year later, nobody cares.

If one reads the actual tapes from the Cockpit Voice Recorders, you will discover that when big trouble happens in the one-in-a-million event, the cockpit heroes are not easily daunted. First they deny there is a problem, then they misdiagnose it, then while the brilliantly designed, computerized airplane is attempting to counter the problem, they fight it until they utter their final famous words, "Oh shit!"

It seems to me that the aircraft are way too advanced for most flight crews when bad things happen. Like a Japanese crew that was warned three times that there was EXTREME turbulence ahead which they would hit when they climbed through 2500 feet. They thanked the advisors but never considered staying on the ground. So they flew calmly into the storm which tore off one of their engines. Then they panicked and did all the wrong things until the "Oh shit."

Other crashes were caused by maintenance mistakes and sometimes just by putting all the fuel on one side of the aircraft. There is one beautiful switch which, when pushed, will abort a landing and do all the things it takes to make the airplane go around for another try at landing. However, if you push that switch by accident, or stupidity, like one pilot, you will really have to fight the airplane to make it land when it thinks you ordered it to go round again. The struggle ended with "Oh Shit!"

Airline pilots always appear cool and nearly all go through their entire career without ever having to follow any emergency procedures spelled out in the many, many manuals. They joke a lot and kid the cabin crew. Dangers are so rare that it's no wonder they don't recognize one when they see one. Some even fly right into a mountain that was on their maps, while they were being cool.

"Oh Sh--!"

Almost all incidents are properly handled and the passengers never know what almost hit them. After all, flight crews are tested and retested, more than heart surgeons. There is a good book, called "The Black Box" by Malcolm Mac Pherson, that describes various accidents and quotes the actual words from the Cockpit Voice Recorders. The confusion in the cockpit before the end is very revealing.

And who could believe that a hundred million dollar airplane and a couple hundred souls would be lost by an airplane washing crew of minimum wage dullards who put some tape over the pitot tubes [air sensor intakes] but forgot to take them off later. The airplane hit the ocean while the altimeter read 10,000 feet.

On the other hand, Boeing had no excuse when a thrust reverser reversed in flight and tore the wing off the fuselage so quickly that there was no time for "Oh shit."

The chaos that occurred on 9/11 was understandable because when one is confronted with an emergency that has never happened before, our mind races through past events looking for an answer that isn't there. The passengers couldn't guess that they were going to die, the FAA controllers had never trained for this, the military and government heads instinctively wanted to call a meeting and get some coffee flowing. They are good at that, and when I worked for the FAA we were quite sharp in our jobs, but, totally a new crisis always brought chaos.

CHAPTER 10 - "DADDY, TELL ME A STORY"

Once upon a time, a long, long time ago, the people on this planet were happy, successful, and prosperous. Some times they couldn't get people to do the dirty work. Nobody wanted to dig ditches, clean rest rooms, and other disagreeable things. So some of their brilliant scientists invented some Robots to do that kind of work. Everyone was happy. Then when there was a shortage of book-keepers, store clerks, and typists they invented Robots to do that. Next they made Robots that could be doctors, nurses, and lawyers. After a long time all factory workers were Robots, they even had Robots making Robots. Finally, the humans had nothing to do so they got into sports in a big way. Football was the biggest, and the champions went at each other with a vengeance.

At last it was the Eastern Hemisphere versus the Western Hemisphere. The competition got as fierce as a war. Then soon it became a war of the East against the West. When the shooting started, people got killed. To keep the bloodshed down, they decided to use Robots for the actual fighting. They instructed a million of them on each side how to shoot. Then they marched them off against the other side.

The two Robot armies met at the border and kept going past each other to kill the people on the other side, as they had been taught. Soon there were no people left so the Robots went to their respective homes. On arriving there they found no one left alive. They decided that the bad Robots on the other side had killed all their beloved people so they went back to the border and attacked the other Robots. They fought so well that soon all the Robots were smashed to bits. The last one left standing looked around and said, "What is the meaning of everything?" He could not answer so he took himself apart, scattering the pieces until he was defunct. The planet was calm."

The little girl asked, "But, Daddy, how did we get here?"

"Well, Honey, while the humans were alive they put a whole lot of garbage and crap into the rivers and oceans. This stuff broke down into cells that had our DNA in it. This floated around for a million years getting sustenance from the ocean water, which has the same chemicals as our blood, except for the salt. These cells formed into groups and then started to specialize. Some accumulated food, some provided propulsion, some took care of sight, and others fought off other groups. Millions of years later a fishlike guy jumped up on the grassy shore and decided to stick around. He and his kind got as big as rats, then dogs, then bigger into monkeys. The monkeys split off into apes and pre-humans. When they developed speech and tools they eventually became US!"

"Daddy, are we going to develop Robots?"

"No, there's a law against it."

"Goodnight, Daddy."

"Good night."

CHAPTER 11- GUILTY BY ASSOCIATION

Some judges put out injunctions against gang action by trying to prohibit them from congregating in groups larger than "two." It doesn't seem to work very well. On the other hand, the term "guilt by association" has always been a no-no in jurisprudence. However if a law were passed to require gangs to obtain a business license or go to jail, then any crime committed by the crime happy gang member would reflect on all of the members and they could all be rounded up and tried for the crime, the court assuming that all crimes were gang sponsored. Naturally, many would say it can't be done because of the "guilt by association" ban. But you and I know that if law makers want to, they can get around any old ban. Just call all gang actions "conspiracy" and the dirty deed would be done.

MORE OF THE SAME OLD, SAME OLD

People without guts or imagination always want "more of the same." That goes for:

BOOK PUBLISHERS - That's why big name authors are urged to write a hundred books, good or bad, they believe they will sell.

AUTO DESIGNERS - The few radical designs that have been brought out in the past have succeeded or failed at about a 50 – 50 rate so we end up with the same old body styles every year. Their ads say "Look at our new car," but it looks like all the rest.

MOVIE PRODUCERS - It's easier to make a sequel than try something new. Producers say they never get into trouble by saying NO to an idea.

MAGAZINE PUBLISHERS - They admit they're gutless. They advise contributors to "read some of our back issues" and you will know what we want. How brave. More of the same please. I tried their method once. I picked a magazine, learned what they were looking for, wrote a two page story and sent it in with an SASE. They thanked me and said that it would be featured in a future issue and enclosed a check for $17.00. I had just paid $32 for IBM typewriter repairs. I did not declare it on my income tax.

MANUFACTURERS - They don't want inventors to send them ideas, especially patented ones. They hope to get by, by making more of the same, unless of course THEY get a new idea (once in a blue moon). There is always the NIH factor. If it's NOT INVENTED HERE, forget it.

ARCHITECTS - "Let's build it like the last one and we won't get in trouble."

AIRLINES - They tell the aircraft manufacturers, "Please do not do anything radical, you'll scare the passengers." That's why most airliners all look alike.

INVESTORS - "No risks please." Just more of the same. So what if it doesn't pay a dividend? Maybe it will double some day. One company had to reduce the dividend because they gave the Chairman of the Board a hundred million dollar bonus.

DON'T LEAVE HOME

People like to stay forever in their home town, home area, home state, home country. A very small percentage of the world ever goes on a foreign vacation. They fear the strange language, foreign money, strange rules and laws. Some Americans feel they are being adventurous if they make a trip to Branson, Mo. or Hawaii before they die. One study showed that most New Yorkers rarely leave an eight block radius around their tenements.

A bit of adventure, such as a vacation that's different, could give a sedentary person something to talk about for years.

I heard a story, maybe not true, about a party where guests would make references to places of the world they had visited. Then the next person would try to top them with his own travelogue. One man sat quietly listening politely to their stories.

Finally, someone addressed him: "Sir, you've been very quiet, have you ever been to an interesting place, maybe overseas?"

He smiled and replied: "Well, let me see. I guess the last trip I made 'overseas' was to the moon." He was one of the Lunar Landing Astronauts.

CHAPTER 12-COULD HE LIGHT A CANDLE? HYPOTHETICALLY?

In a hypothetical question, any situation can be posited. In other words, no one can say "No way."

WHAT IF some world body such as the U.N. got together all the leaders in the many religions and it was agreed by all to try a demo of God's love for this world. WHAT IF on a New Year's Eve by the Christian Calendar, at exactly midnight, Greenwich (England) time, at a place agreed upon such as the Taj Mahal, Eiffel Tower, Vatican, Times Square or elsewhere, all believers around the world would pray at the same time, same minute, for God(s) to light a candle at the designated spot. It could be just a tiny birthday cake candle, but it would be visible by television and computers everywhere. If there is a God(s), would he light the candle? Or would he be too busy someplace else? After all, the center of the universe seems to be over a dozen billion light years away. If your God is limited by the laws of physics and math, it would take a while for Him to get the request to perform at the candle lighting ceremony. But if you have invented a God who can DO ANYTHING, then HE could do the trick from anywhere HE is at the time. Would He(she) or wouldn't He(she)?????

Some theologians say that the believers have two choices:

ONE: God can do anything but he does not care to.

TWO: God wants to help us but He can't.

Pick the choice you like.

Getting back to the hypothetical, would the little candle light—or not?

After all, Deities are what we say they are.

"How many troops do you have?"

"You don't have a 'need to know'."

"What's your authority for deciding that?"

"I don't have a 'need to know'."

"Oh."

CHAPTER 13 - GEOPOLITICAL DISAPPOINTMENTS

His name was Dakota Rockefeller and in his senior year at Princeton, he applied to the U.S. State Department for a position where he could apply his studies in World Politics and Political Sciences. To his surprise, he was accepted. His grades had been good—but not that good. His family was influential, but not—oh well….

He reported to the designated building in D.C. and was assigned a cubicle. He studied bulletins for a few days and then, on his first Friday afternoon, the department manager's secretary came and told him that the Head Honcho wanted to see him. He hurried.

"Rockefeller, listen up. Everyone is gone and you're all I got. Go rent a full dress suit and shoes to represent your country at…" He looked at the invite, "the Lithuanian Independence Ball. I'll order a limo to pick you up about eight. Now go and don't screw up!"

As he entered the tall doors of the mansion, he tried not to stare at the exquisite art on the walls of the block long foyer. He noticed several couples who were enjoying a last smoke before entering the Ball Room. The murmur of a waltz was beginning. So he lit a cigarette, no hurry.

Then the earth stood still. The next couple through the door consisted of a short white-haired elderly gentleman wearing the red sash of diplomatic rank. With him was a six foot Miss Universe with blonde hair piled high into a diamond tiara. Her long neck carried a matching diamond necklace that could pay off a national debt. Her chest was trying to escape the long white satin evening gown.

A butler appeared and whispered something about a telephone call into the old man's ear. The two men left together. A little drool dropped from the Rockefeller lip. The young lady opened a tiny, diamond studded evening bag and removed a case and slowly selected a silver tipped cigarette. A bell rang in his brain and he realized he must do something.

Fumbling in his pocket he found his lighter and moved close enough to extend it to her presence.

Without looking at him, she used the flame to ignite and smoke a single puff. He realized that social protocol required him to make some kind of remark, after which she would reject him and the earth could resume its rotation. He deemed it would be less tiring for her if he offered an inane remark, so that then her rejection would be totally fitting.

He assumed a familiar tone and said:" Buy you a beer?"

She took a longer puff, then staring at her cigarette, her eyes flickering for a half second in his direction, she paused a lifetime.

Slowly she said: "No, beer makes me fart."

CHAPTER 14 - FEED THE POOR BEFORE ALL ELSE?

Whenever a really big project is proposed, like sending a man to the moon, or Mars, or beyond, some group is sure to protest. "Think of all the starving babies that money would feed." What should we prefer, Feat or Famine?

As my grandfather is supposed to have said, "There's much to be said on both sides." He was deep, and still is. And remember, there are always more poor people than big spenders so you should never put these ideas to a vote.

Let's analyze a few big money items:

The Taj Mahal. It is surrounded by plenty of poor people.

The Statue of Liberty was once called the Statute of Limitations.

The Washington Monument. It's in a welfare neighborhood.

The Lincoln Memorial. His freed slaves became poor.

Columbus' Ships. This political boondoggle cost plenty.

The Great Wall of China. Expensive but didn't stop bad guys.

La Tour Eiffel. The elite protested and the poor went hungry.

L'Arc de Triomphe. Napoleon spent a bundle for his glory.

The Sphinx. No one knows what it cost or who paid for it.

All the Castles of the World. Built by rich rulers or money men.

Today, a nuclear submarine, aircraft carrier, stealth bomber, or a trip to the moon costs more than enough to feed all the poor on earth for a day or two. BUT, what about all the jobs these projects provided for Asians, Europeans, Africans, and Americans.

One thing is certain, the prospective contractors and their workers have more clout than all the starving babies will ever have.

So, let's spend the money to build a hotel on Mars. Think of what it would do to our economy, think of the bragging rights. So what if the hotel has no atmosphere?

CHAPTER 15 - THE DUMB BELL PLANETS, DUMB AND DUMBER

In a galaxy far, far away there were planets with people just like us except that they had fur instead of clothes and they walked with their knuckles on the ground. An Engineer named One-Oh-One [he was conceived in Algebra 101] had just bought a new car and called his best friend, Hairy, to tell him about it.

Their home planet(s) consisted of two planets, side by side, touching each other and revolving around each other at an energetic pace. This spinning provided enough centrifugal force to keep the two giants from crushing each other. The area where they co-joined was quite a tourist attraction. Loopy local lore had it that where the lands were only about ten feet apart, and quite dark, the gravity was so strong you could cut it with a knife and bottle it. In fact, tourists paid good coins for a can of gravity.

101: "Hey, Hairy, I'll be right over to show you my new car. It's one of those low flyers and I can't wait to try it on the highway. We can drive it to the Gravity Center, it's only a thousand poles, are you with me?"

Hairy: "He is!"

As they cruised along the highway, 101 explained, "This thing takes up half the road 'cause it is shaped like a thick wing and has flight controls. With a clear road I can go 80, lift it up and glide for quite a ways. And I bought the special air tank called The Blo Jo. You just push a button and you can fly ten times as far. The air tank gets refilled as you drive, understand?"

Hairy: "He does."

As the space between the planets became less and less, they saw souvenir stands everywhere. As the space between worlds got down to thrice the height of a person, they could see teen-agers using ladders to jump to the other world. It was quite difficult to know the name of the planet you were standing on. The ancient explorers had decreed that the planet facing the "sun" should be named Hard Ball and the other one Soft Ball. Ergo, the two tumblers had a name change every, well, every so often.

Suddenly their progress was halted by a gate guarded by some sort of armed soldiers. One demanded, "This is a toll road; to pass, you must pay a hundred tokens."

101 was chagrined, "Well, we will just do a 360 and go back the way we came."

The Highwayman grinned, "There is another gate behind you."

Hairy spoke up, "Well we won't pay!"

The biggest bad guy nodded to the others. They gathered around the car and lifted it up above their heads into the neutral zone, half way between worlds.

"Now you will stay there until you pay."

101 looked at Hairy and whispered, "We have no option."

Hairy mumbled, "You brought an option."

"What option?"

"You know, optional equipment, the blower."

"Oh, the optional gizmo I was conned into buying, the Air Tank and Jet."

"Yes. That red button."

101 punched the red button and twisted the control wheel at the same time. The jet blew away the highwaymen and twisted the car back towards the way they had come.

As they headed home, Hairy asked, "What was it the Wise Old Geezer said about playing Hard Ball and Soft Ball?"

I believe he said, "When worlds collide, it's best to stay out of the crotch."

CHAPTER 16 - NONSEQUITORS

Enlightened religionists (an oxymoron) try to tell us that people born in a laboratory dish have no soul. They say that an angel inserts the soul at the instant that the sperm hits the egg: conception. It has also been said that it takes a million sperm to find the egg because they do not stop to ask directions.

Conceptions, immaculate and otherwise, often occur on Friday nights in lover's lane near the high school. And if there are fifty cars parked there, you can be certain that there are fifty angels perched on fence posts nearby, watching and waiting for that split second event to occur.

The angels have no problem locating these places because of the loud discordant music emanating from hundreds of speakers powered by the amplifiers of the car radios. The angels refer to this as "soul" music.

CHAPTER 17 - MNEMONICS

If you ever have occasion to want to remember the names of the six smallest countries in Europe, and who hasn't, here is a handy dandy memory helper: SSMMALL-V   It sounds like 'small' so it is easy to remember in itself. This is important in memory aids. Because first you have to remember the memory aid.

S = Switzerland

S = San Marino [surrounded by Italy]

M = Monaco

M = Malta

A = Andorra [between France and Spain]

L = Luxemburg

L = Lichtenstein

V = Vatican

To this list you could probably add a place called The Knights of Malta which is a separate country but consists of just one building, a hospital, I think.

Whenever you are trying to remember the names of our nine planets and keep them in order as they relate to the sun, it is easy if you just memorize this simple sentence: My Very Enterprising Mother Joined Several Unusual Night Patrols.

IF you can remember that simple sentence, you'll see that the first letter in each word is the same as the first letter in the name of a planet and in the right position.

M = Mercury

V = Venus

E = Earth

M = Mars

J = Jupiter

S = Saturn

U = Uranus

N = Neptune

P = Pluto

Now you can forget Astrology and learn Astronomy.

CHAPTER 18 - FAMOUS SONGS THAT DIDN'T MAKE IT

If I took you to a dog fight, you'd probably win.

If my nose was full of nickels, I'd blow it all on you.

I used to kiss your lips but it's all over now.

Let me crawl you sweetheart.

Here's a quarter, go call somebody who cares.

If your phone don't ring, you know it's me.

Here's a dollar for a condom so you won't reproduce yourself.

I miss you almost as much as if you were with me.

I can't climb into an upper berth so, to you, sweetheart, Aloha.

While I was out getting hammered, you were home getting nailed.

I gave her a diamond and she gave me the finger.

If I owed someone an ugly woman and he wouldn't take you, I don't know when I could pay him off.

CHAPTER 19 - HOW TO CATCH A WILD HORSE

Horse type animals that were native to North America died out some thousands of years ago, but some of their bones can be found in places like the La Brea Tar Pits in Los Angeles along with Mammoths, Mastodons, Giant Bison, Giant Lions etc.

When Native Americans first saw European horses with explorers such as Cortez, they thought they were big deer.

Later, an Indian's wealth was noted by how many horses he owned. Poor Indian boys found out that you could chase a horse for days until it gave up. A horse has to stop and eat grass once in a while but an Indian could put some jerky in his belt and follow the horse as long as it was necessary.

A visiting European General once observed, back in the 1800's, that a mounted Indian troop was "excellent light cavalry."

CHAPTER 20 - HOW TO TORTURE A PERSON

If you have captured a known terrorist, murderer, rapist, or child molester you cannot punch them or be nasty enough to cause a bruise because they have more rights than their victims. That's the LAW as written by the courts, especially the Supremes.

I found out by accident that if you stand behind a sitting person and put an open handed slap on the top of their head, they will be very surprised and sometimes disoriented. They will hope you will not do it again.

Here you are in a position of power, and handcuffs are suggested. The target never knows when the next clap-to-the-crown is coming and if the force of the cranial whap is increased each time and the blow comes at irregular intervals, the result is conducive to insanity, temporary or otherwise. It is devastating to even the most serene composure. And it leaves no marks.

If you wish to demonstrate this in a semi-clinical manner in the comfort of your own home or office, have a friend, or even just an acquaintance who admires you, participate. While you're sitting ask them to stand behind you and instruct them to slap you smartly on the top of your head at a time of their choosing. And then have them do it again when they feel like it. Twice; no more.

You will find it to be non-habit-forming. Be sure to arrange in advance that you will TAKE TURNS! Thus you will each be gentler and so preserve the friendship.

In a police atmosphere the procedure would probably be found to be intolerable by the recipient and should leave no marks, scars, bruises, or other visible evidence of custodial abuse.

CHAPTER 21 - EXORCISM & CIRCUMCISION

Two rites that can make a wrong.

Occasionally someone dies during an exorcism or as a result of a circumcision. That is unforgivable. Religion is supposed to be a harmless, benign game of pretend that features various gods, goddesses, devils, and devilettes. These are those invisible and folklorical olden guys and gals up in the sky that always need money.

When you donate it makes you have a warm feeling inside and some of your donation may even go to someone who needs it. But don't forget that the administrative cost part of the collection comes first, naturally.

Exorcisors:

If a licensed cleric finds that someone is inhabited by a demon or devil and if he can prove it in a laboratory or a court of law, then a legal permit should be issued to a board certified theologian with a proven record of demon/devil demolition. This would require a legal definition of such creatures' existence as defined by the appropriate civil law.

Circumcision:

Folklore has it that this religious rite of mutilation dates back to the murky mists of time as a hygienic procedure. This devious dogma tries to cover up the real reason which was to discourage boys from playing "pocket pool" or "spanking the monkey." These are just two of the hundreds of euphemisms invented to describe male masturbation. Nature provides males with a tender, sensitive member to promote the propagation of the race and the pursuit of happiness.

During urination and bathing some handling of the device is necessary, thus resulting in further massaging which in turn reduces excess testosterone and sex drive. Although various primitive tribes in the general Mediterranean area became convinced that gods or goddesses had decreed the foreskin snipping ritual for health reasons, research revealed that this minor mutilation is more dangerous than a dirty dick.

However, no amount of member mutilation seems to reduce the constant production of semen and thus the boy's sex drive continues unabated. The removal of the protective skin does remove part of the sensitivity in the dick-head and thus part of the pleasure of intercourse, but since there is a constant over production of these life- giving juices, the population growth continues as expected and required.

Note to all species: REPRODUCE OR DIE OUT!

CHAPTER 22 - DON'T BE A FANATIC

One should try not to be fanatical about anything, whether it is politics, religion, fashion, food, or finances. Fanatics seem to have one little part of their brains that is retarded just enough to make them see such subjects with a big bad bias.

They say that after a good life, death is okay.

Nobody can know the meaning of life until they've had a life.

A man from Iowa finally made the trip of his dreams. He visited the Eiffel Tower, the Vatican, and the Taj Mahal. When he got home, his friends asked: "How was the food?"

Marriage was an invention of man and can be reinvented any way we want. But speaking of Gays marrying, why would a Gay man want to marry a Lesbian?

GOOD GAMBLING

Someone should build or convert a casino where you pay $50 to enter, but the house has no edge. For instance:

Blackjack — If the dealer goes over 21, the players who have also gone over 21 get a "push." They neither win nor lose; their bets stay for the next hand.

Roulette — The table has 36 numbers plus zero and double zero, so a winner would be paid 38 to one.

Craps — The table would have a diagram on the surface where anyone could play WITH the house.

Poker — The dealer would not take out a house cut for every hand.

NOTE: In all cases, the dealers would welcome tips.

I would rush to play in such a place and so would millions of others.

OUTSOURCING OUR JOBS

Last week I made a long distance call to New Delhi, India, and it didn't cost me a thing. My TV was acting up so I looked on the guarantee and called the 800 number given. A nice spoken young lady answered and we had a nice conversation about my contract which had expired twenty minutes before. I like to guess at foreign accents but she didn't seem to have one. I asked her about the weather and she said it was quite dark outside so I asked her where she was. She said, "New Delhi." It didn't cost me a cent but then I wondered about the American who had lost his job so that a big corporation could save a few cents. If the Indians can save us so much money, maybe we should use them for the executives of that corporation. And our greedy politicians who depend on those companies for reelection.

To obtain my last three positions, I had to take an I.Q. test. Wouldn't that be a good requirement when running for public office? We could find out who are the dumbshits.

When kids have trouble reading the words, they don't notice that they come in sentences.

A FUTURE SENSE

There is a sense that has yet to be discovered…it is the one used by schools of fish and flocks of birds to turn and zoom as one, even though there are hundreds of them. Another example of this "sense" was made by a study of a little bird in England, called the "Blue Tit." When milkmen delivered bottles of milk door-to-door, sometimes in the winter, the cream on top would freeze and thereby push up the stiff paper cap. The Blue Tit found out that the frozen cream was delicious and even when the weather was balmier; they learned to pry up the cardboard cap and drink the cream.

The discoverer of this boon must have told all his friends as soon they were all doing the dastardly deed.

BUT…Soon the Blue Tits of Holland were doing the same trick! No Blue Tit was ever able to fly across the English Channel, so how did they tell their Dutch Uncles and cousins about this bonanza? There must be a sense, unknown to us as yet, that some animals use to communicate. Maybe it is the same mysterious sense used by human mind readers when they're lucky; it doesn't always work for humans.

Many people claim that their pets have an unusual sense that is not explained by conventional ways. One man said that his dog always was waiting at the door for him, and whenever he leaves his job early, the dog senses it and moves to the front door just when he's leaving the office. It is probably, I guess, the same sense the flocks and the fishes use for their amazing formation flying. A millennium ago, no one was utilizing electricity and who knows, some day we may be using this unknown sense. This would make obsolete telephones, e-mail, lying, secrets and adultery.

CHAPTER 23 - FAMILY PLANS

Spain has a minus population gain, Canada still welcomes immigrants (some times terrorists)and Catholic "speakers" advocate "mass" production of babies disirregardless [not a real word] of the ability to feed them. Clothing, housing, and education are luxuries to these types. No country has yet to come up with a licensing plan for couples to make babies. This might require paperwork to establish one's ability to afford and properly tend one's herd.

My grandmother, nee Silka Fink Schneckloth, had thirteen children, but her husband, Thomas, was wealthy, and besides in the 1870s, our country needed population to till the black fertile soil of Iowa. Grandpa came from Sleswig-Holstein, Germany at the age of four. His father was carrying a sack of gold coins and landed in New Orleans to buy farming equipment. He proceeded by river steamer up the Mississippi to Davenport, Iowa. He went inland about 10 miles and bought 120 acres for about $2.00 each. Why not borrow money from a bank and buy more at such a low price? The answer: The interest rate was 40%!!!

Note: Out of those 13 children, four died in the Flu epidemic while they were quite young. When I was a bratty little kid I thought my grandmother was an ugly tyrant, but years later when I saw her photo in a book in the public library I saw she had been a real beauty. Amazing!

DON'T LOSE YOUR HEAD

J.I. Guillotine, a French Doctor, invented the head chopper machine because he thought it would be more humane than the executioner's axe, especially during his learning curve. It became familiar to many of the crowned heads of the early 1800s. But how humane do you want to be while chopping off your enemy's head? Just because the face had a blank stare when it dropped into the basket, doesn't mean it wasn't feeling pain, or remorse, or maybe it wanted to apologize for having somehow impugned someone's honor.

Do the chopees die instantly? Maybe, maybe not. You have to choke someone for maybe half a minute in order to cut off both the blood to the brain and the air to the lungs. IF this is true, it would give the head person in the basket time to wonder about such things as: Who will look after my: canary, gold fish, spouse, bank account, mistress, children, dirty pictures, hidden gold, horses, etc.? For Lady detachees it might be: That roast in the oven, Am I pregnant? Who's the father? I could kill that Andre -- oops, gotta go.

PEOPLE'S PROBLEMS SOLVED ELSEWHERE

HEALTH CARE

In many industrialized countries, you get a choice. Pay the Doc of your choice or go to a Government salaried Doc. No one is denied care.

HOUSING

Here again, most places give you the option: Buy or rent the place of your choice, or live in a Government operated building. In the latter, no funny business is allowed: Be neat, be friendly, and be quiet. Non-conformists can try another country.

FOOD

Food stamps and meal tickets are notorious for being used to trade in dope, etc. Welfare checks often leave the kids hungry and the rent unpaid. Soup kitchens seem to hurt self esteem but why not GET A JOB?

ILLEGALS

Most mature countries require all to carry an identity card that a computer can read in a fraction of a second. Their police are required to keep tabs on tourists, visiting students, guest workers etc. If your visa has expired, they will let you know, and, they know where you are.

GUNS UNLIMITED

I once met the late Senator Cranston in a Ralph's Market where he was shaking hands with the shoppers. I asked him: "How come you are eighty times more likely to be shot here than in England?"

He replied quickly: "Don't mention guns, the NRA will get me."

The NRA really stands for the National Riflemakers Association. Gun makers make such huge profits on revolvers and automatic pistols that they can afford to BRIBE every Senator and Congressman. THEY call it lobbying. Our lawmakers don't even dare vote to ban machine guns, machine pistols, and other automatic weapons. Most other nations do not allow bribing of lawmakers. But our Supreme Court says it's not really wrong.

SIMPLE SOLUTIONS

These are usually called "simplistic" because our lawyers want to obfuscate everything and snarl things up so that we have to hire them to explain it to us.

DROP OUTS

I tell young people that if they don't finish their education, most of life will go over their heads. Some agree, some say: "Who gives a damn?"

In conversations, on TV sitcoms, dramas, movies, and news, most clever lines require a little comprehension to get the benefit of the bon mots. Euphemisms, clichés, and references to history, geography, government, the many sciences, and the multitude of foreign phrases slide right over the heads of those standing in the hole of chronic mental lassitude and sloth.

Note: Sloths are arboreal South American mammals who only move a few feet a year. It is believed that when Noah sent out telegrams to all the animals on earth to come in pairs [heterosexuals only] to the Ark, the Sloths got the message but they are still on their way.

Question: Why is the Ark always drawn with "pointy" ends? Whither goest it?

HOW TO MEET SOME ONE

Most single people would like to meet a nice specimen of the opposite sex. So what is the best way? The time tested way is to get drunk in a bar.

CHAPTER 24 - MOTORCYCLES

Motorcycle Mechanic: "Hey, Doc, you're a surgeon, right? Well we both do the same work, we take things apart and fix them. How come you get paid fifty times more then me?"

Doctor: "Try taking one apart while it's running."

"Mr. Kebob, what is your first name?"

"I don't have one."

'Sheesh!"

"That's a good one, I'll take it."

Opera and esoteric art were invented to make poor people feel dumb.

THE U.S. OF LUIGI

500 years ago a Mrs. Vespucci was about to have a baby. Her friend asked, "What will you name him if it's a boy?"

She replied: "I would like to name him Luigi but uncle Americus has all the money in the family."

He later became a famous map maker and the Americas were named after him. If his mother had stayed with her original desires, we would now be known as the United States of Luigi.

Les Etats Unis   Los Estados Unidos   Der Verinikten Staden [?]

BABY LICENSES

One has to have a license to drive a car, cut hair, own a dog, and get married. Is it not more important to beget babies? People should have to take a written test, physical exam, and maybe even a road test to bring future welfare recipients into our oh so regulated world. Many of us would not be here. You readers excepted of course.

GLOBAL WARMING

People say that the current global warming is very bad for the planet, the ocean will rise and flood coastal towns etc. One low island in the Pacific is supposed to have already disappeared. But About 150 years ago someone started measuring temperatures around the earth to get a world average. And it turns out that the world average today is about one degree F. cooler today than it was 150 years ago. What cooks?

MIRACLES

Miracles are something that happens but are not understood by you. Maybe to someone else who understands the event, it is commonplace.

Marriage is like a 50 course dinner with the dessert first.

Feed a brain, starve a fool.

Kids: Flipping burgers is not beneath your dignity, it is an opportunity.

Kids: If you think the teacher is tough, wait till you have a boss.

Kids: Be nice to Nerds, chances are you'll be working for one.

Kids: There are two kinds of people in the world: Nerds and Turds. Try to be a Nerd.

Kids: Before you can clean up the rain forests you have to clean up your room.

Kids: Your boss won't try to help you find yourself, just be where he thinks you are.

Kids: Why do kid singers try to eat the microphone?

OCTUPI

Some day octopi will take over the earth. They can move eight arms independently and at the same time.

FENCES

If we built a twelve foot electrified fence along our Mexican border, we would have to raise the minimum wage and hire the people on welfare. WHAT?

CHAPTER 25 - HOW TO MAKE AN ATOM BOMB

Back during the days of WWII, the scientists in Los Alamos, New Mexico, came up with two different ways to make radioactive material reach a critical mass. I believe they used both methods to make two bombs which were exported to Japan. They were delivered about four years after the sneak attack on Hawaii.

To understand the term "critical mass," let's visualize a grapefruit with atomic particles shooting out in all directions. Now if you increase these discharges to the point where the grapefruit doesn't have enough skin to handle the traffic, something's gotta give, it must explode.

Then the problem becomes how to make such a mass for a bomb without blowing yourself up in the process. They came up with two different ways. In the first, you make half the critical amount in two different balls, place two cannon barrels facing each other, and the when both cannons fire at exactly the same time, the two globs meet and blow up. If they did it any slower they would ruin each other on the way to the meeting.

The other way was to have a ball of stuff [Uranium 235] diluted so that it was not yet critical. Then you surrounded it with something like TNT which, when detonated, could squeeze the gunk down to a critical mass.

In fractured Deutsch :

An A-Bomb = ein louden boomen

An H-Bomb = ein louden boomen alles kaput

Several nuclear physicists worked on ways to refine uranium down to the point where a bomb could be made. One guy came up with a machine like a very tall refrigerator that would groan for a few days and produce a speck of the needed stuff that was almost too small to see. When the leader saw the results he said "Now all we need is three hundred thousand of these machines to make a bomb a week."

Factories were built in several places; the one in the Northwest was really colossal and worked entirely without any people in it, too radioactive.

By the time the Japanese got their surprise, the Atomic Energy facilities covered more floor space than all of the American automobile industry combined.

And it only cost two billion dollars

Or as that old Roman, Gluteus Maximus, used to say, "If you take life too seriously, it's no longer FUN."

CHAPTER 26 - BURNING DOWN YOUR MASTER'S HOUSE

Some ex-reporter wrote a book with this title. It reminded me of a historical comment in James Michener's book, The Caribbean. He stated that during the period when most of these islands were colonized by Europeans who had brought in African slaves to work the sugar cane fields, Haiti was the most wealthy and prosperous of them all. The Africans were well housed, well fed, and well clothed. They were happy and their French masters who lived in mansions were happy.

Then outsiders from other islands came and convinced the Haitian blacks to revolt for freedom, kill their oppressors, and burn down their mansions They did just that and Haiti has been on the skids ever since.

Now Haiti is the poorest nation in the Caribbean. I guess this means that being FREE does not provide the management skills required for an agrarian society.

The Dominican Republic occupies the eastern half of the island of Hispaniola, while Haiti occupies the western part. The Dominicans seem to be doing well and with the same natural resources. This makes us wonder about the benefits of revolting.

Hispanic revolutionaries in Central and South America often try to justify their actions by pointing to our own revolution circa 1776. BUT, our revolters were prosperous business men and other pillars of the colonies who gave their wealth and lives for freedom. Latin American revolters, when successful, merely install a new line of looters.

Joke: It is said that bull fighting is the number one sport in Latin America.

Many believe it's revolting. That's not true, revolting is the number two sport.

Note: Mother Nature made women smaller than men so that they wouldn't beat them to death.

CHAPTER 27 - YOUR INTEREST IN BANKS

A If you borrow from a friend and agree to pay him normal interest, the most he can charge you is the same as a bank. Right? WRONG! Only banks are allowed to gouge. Private parties are limited to about 16%.

B If you sign up for a new credit card without reading ALL the ten pages of fine print, and if they say therein that the interest rate is FIXED forever, they can't raise it. Right? WRONG! Try missing a payment and it might go up to — whoa, 35%?

C Banks are regulated by state and federal agencies that write laws to protect us and then enforce the laws. Right? WRONG! Bankers and their lobbyists write the laws and then see that they are not enforced. Described on the show, 60 Minutes.

CHAPTER 28 - OLDE LYRICS

She said, "Dear, I'm dying, and I haven't been true."

He said, "Dear, I know you're dying, cause I poisoned you."

Now she's pushing up daisies,

Hoping they'll tell you to,

Never to cheat your husband,

You'll be pushing up daisies, too.

They used to make jokes about men lying in their coffins. It may have been one of the few times that they were all dressed up. Around about 1925 someone wrote a song about it.

When you're all dressed up and no where to go,

Life seems weary, dreary and slow,

My heart has ached and bled,

For the tears I've shed,

But there's no place to go,

Unless I go back to bed.

EDDY HILL

I've had a long sad life and whenever I go,

To that peaceful spot where the violets grow,

There'll be a nice white stone,

Where it's written below,

He was all dressed up but no place to go.

Unless, of course, you prefer cremation.

When a man named Paul Gary Beck, Karuk Tribal Chairman, was interviewed, he was quoted as saying, "For 10,000 years or more our people have lived along the Klamath River in this peaceful, isolated place. We believe that the world began here and that this is the cradle of civilization and that we were the first people on earth." I have heard similar words from tribesmen in central Africa and elsewhere, including New Yorkers and Parisians. Paleontologists have found that the Africans were the closest to the truth.

Our old High School principle once said, "If COOL is the only adjective you know,

You are probably a very dull conversationalist.

Some in Texas say that George W. Bush is all hat and no cows.

The BIG BANG must have happened when God had an orgasm.

Your brain just wants to have fun. So it welcomes all drugs.

I once attended a wedding celebration party where everyone was drinking and laughing it up, including me. One nice looking young lady was exhorting a circle of listeners about her theories on life. She declaimed that all of us and the earth and the universe were not really real. We were just figments of imagination and that nothing was even here. She ranted on for quite a while and finally when she stopped for air, I asked, "If nothing is real and none of this is happening, then if I put my right hand on your left breast, it won't really happen."

She said, "You do, and I'll kill you!"

If the Real Estate argument between the Palestinians and the Israelis is not solved by outsiders, they will bomb and retaliate for the next hundred years.

Two hundred years ago, my ancestors were slaves in Germany. Where do I apply for my reparations?

When I was in the sixth grade, our teacher explained to us that the earth was divided into three zones:

Artic

Temperate

Tropical

She said that the people living in the Artic zone had such a struggle to stay alive that they didn't have time for schooling, art or entertainment.

She said that the people in the Tropics always had warm weather, so they hunted, fished, and raised herds of domestic animals. There was plenty of natural food around so they were content to take things easy.

She said that in the temperate zone, one had to work hard in summer to prepare for winter. They had to build houses to withstand the cold, make clothing that would allow them outdoors, and develop agriculture to amass food. Those who were lazy did not do well and usually did not reproduce, and eventually most of us were born with the ambition to work from dawn till dusk. This still left us time to develop the arts, education, science, and many other civil pursuits.

CHAPTER 29 - NEW PRODUCTS

Bird Laxative

Non-alcoholic Vodka

Lobster Helper

Yellow Ty-D-Bol

Seeing-Eye Giraffes

Intermittent Headlights

Kosher Communion Wafers

Chick Repellent

Inflatable Dart Board

Suzuki Rollover Wheels

IN THE NEWS

The new aircraft carrier will be named the USS Cost Over Run instead of its original name, the USS Powder Keg.

A new Post Office was dedicated in the town of Witness Protection Corners, Ind.

A local lad, Bubba Boynton, has dropped out of high school to write a book. The title of the new book will be, "THE ARISTOCRACY OF TALENT AND MERIT."

A man, who is a dress designer, called a press conference to announce his new fabric which will cloak all of any woman's curves. The twenty reporters took him outside and kicked the shit out of him.

CHAPTER 30 - BIG BIGOTS

Most bigots have a beautiful future behind them.

A guy named Rousseau said, "Marriage has civil consequences without which it would be impossible for society itself to subsist." He obviously had never studied the history of mankind and its animal predecessors. If you go back about five million years you find that mankind alternately prospered and sputtered as they reproduced our ancestors without the benefit of clergy or judge. Then, about eight or ten thousand years ago, marriage as a property right was invented. So, for the first 98% of our existence we "subsisted" without it.

We had sort of successful families without any "rite." And any Gays that were around were not labeled just because they had no natural appetite for the opposite sex. Later, we developed nice names for the confirmed bachelor and spinster. We just enjoyed their company.

So-called conservationists spend their time worrying about possible extinction of species. But 90% of all species that ever lived [plants and animals] became extinct before the advent of man. A lot of this can be blamed on the giant rock that hit the earth in the area of Yucatan a zillion years ago. As species are still evolving, some will thrive and some will die. The gators, crocs and turtles don't seem to care. They say they've been here for at least 120 million years. Maybe that's why they're so ornery.

Mountains don't last forever either. A peak seems to lose about three inches every hundred years. Some say that our Rocky Mountains were here at least twice. They wear down to zero in about six million years [15,000 feet divided by 25 times 100]. Every so often the big tectonic plates under the Pacific Ocean push, grunt, and groan, and then we get a new set of mountains, which again start to disintegrate at three inches a year.

Archeologists dig it.

Anthropology is a science where you study people. It takes four years to learn how. I met an old lady in Kuala Lumpur who said she was one of these. But she pronounced it "AnthropoLOGY." She scared me.

Daughter: "Mother, I'm pregnant."

Mother: "Who's the father?"

Daughter: "God."

Mother: "Yeah, sure, just wait 'til your father gets home."

Did the Creator of the Universe work 16 billion years on His project and then go to an insignificant little village in the sands of the Middle East to father a son? And He stood by while some local politicians killed him? Some of the leaders of the other great religions question the idea.

In Cuba, the most hip song is, "Row, row, row your boat."

In Alabama they don't say, "Once upon a time." They say, "You're not going to believe this shit."

Are our leaders really the best we've got?

Hunters should have to take a test when they apply for a hunting license to make sure they are smarter than the animals.

The Mayor of Hiroshima should not be criticized for using the F word. He was quite proper when he said, "What the fuck was THAT?"

Religion sometimes gets in the way of morality.

When did our kids take the tunes out of music? Maybe the loud drum soloing is to drown out the singing. The drummers are taking us back to the jungle.

A Biologist writes that when a woman's plumbing presents an egg into position, if she does not fertilize it, she aborts it.

CHAPTER 31 - GOD DOES NOT MAKE MISTAKES

But sometimes Nature does.

Examples:

Our last millennium only lasted 999 years [year 1001 to 1999].

The reversal of the magnetic fields on Mars probably let all the air and water escape.

There are legless lizards.

We have flightless birds.

There are blind fish.

We have birds that steal [Bower birds of New Guinea].

There are Lesbians etc.

There are Platypuses.

We have deaf-mutes.

There at least 500 Indian women without nipples. [Indian Nippleless 500]

There are gay animals.

Tapioca Pudding.

Bosses without hearts.

Edsels.

Pedal-philes [bike lovers?]

Big-boned snakes.

Colliding galaxies.

15,000 babies born every hour.

CHAPTER 32 - FIFTY CENTS

As a freshman in 1938, I was a member of the Rifle Team and was awarded a sweater with the numerals 1942 sewed thereon. In the spring of 1942 and 1943 I became the Emcee of the annual Engineering "smoker." On stage I told jokes and interviewed the MECCA queen candidates. In 1943, in preparation for a joke, I took my numeral sweater to a tailor and him revise the numbers from 1942 to 1492. I planned to open my jacket during my act and comment that I was the oldest student in town.

The evening was a riotous success, but I forgot to open my jacket for the big gag display... No one ever saw the joke I was planning, and the next week I left for the Army Air Corps. That was fifty cents down the drain! Maybe my mother was right when, as a boy, she named me "The Absent Minded Professor."

I'm going to write a Diet Book where you are required to eat nothing but pie for a year. The book will be on the Best Seller list for a long time.

KIDS: You are not "entitled." You have to earn it. Start out by loving yourself and what you do. Life is entertaining—enjoy it.

New York, N.Y.

New York has two kinds of residents: Millionaires and Blue Collar. And a lot of them speak some English.

"You're a slut."

"You're a tramp."

"You're a whore."

"You can't coordinate."

"Oh, don't say that."

If you ASSUME you live at the center of the most important spot on earth then it's logical to ASSUME that God listens to you.

When the clerk says, "Have a nice day." You can reply with, "Have a nice hour."   Or better yet, say, "Have a nice cliché."

CHAPTER 33 - PROFESSIONALS

"I'M A PROFESSIONAL GARBAGE COLLECTOR"

People seem to think that if they work for pay, they are professionals. I suppose that's true for such as baseball players. Hookers claim to be in the "oldest profession." What they mean is the oldest paying JOB. Most people think that if they do a good job of whatever they're doing, they're being professional. It's snuck into the dialectics to the point that everyone accepts it.

When I entered a scientific field in a University, we were lectured that there were only four professions:

Medicine

Science

Law

Theology

Each of these has many subsections. Medicine has – Dentistry, Nursing, Chiropractors, Naturopathy, Hypnotism, Herbology, Veterinary, and many more.

Science includes Engineering, Architecture, Astronomy, Physics, Geology, Paleontology and many more.

Engineering is the only one of the four professions where one is not allowed to GUESS.

Law has many subdivisions that I don't understand.

Theology probably has as many. I once read that many historical biblical researchers don't believe in a Supreme Being. I'd guess that would make them more neutral and dispassionate on the subject.

So if your son says he's going to turn Pro, he's probably talking about his favorite sport. If your teen age daughter says she's going to turn Pro, you had better sit down and talk.

IN JESUS' STEPS

If you visit Jerusalem today, a guide will show you exactly where Jesus Christ, the Nazarene carried the cross on his way to his execution. Millions of tourists have done the same, without the nasty ending, of course.

James Michener conducts formidable research when writing his books. In one, I believe it was The Source, he describes how the wife of Emperor Constantine, the first real Christian King, visited Jerusalem and asked to see where Jesus walked. One group insisted it was on certain streets while other groups insisted that he had used other paths (probably past their shops). Since there appeared to be no agreement, she decided to settle the matter once and for all and by a Royal Decree. She designated certain paths as the official route and so the puzzle was solved for all time to come. Forever. Unless of course, someone comes along with a Time Machine and visits the area in the year of 33AD, plus or minus a few years, the date is not certain. A prologue in my old Bible says that He probably died on Jan. 4.

Where's the Emperor's wife when you need her?

Some writer once wrote a letter to Einstein and asked him, "If there is a God, wouldn't He have to have had a designer?"

Einstein answered, "Yes."

So, even God has to answer to a higher power.

THE WORLD'S HAPPIEST PEOPLE

The happiest and most lovable people in the world must be those who believe in EASY GOING INDIFFERENTISM. I'll bet they live longer and prosper more.

CHAPTER 34 - WIT

We "child-proofed" our house but they still get in.

If you would like to go back to your youth, think about Algebra.

Never slap a man who's chewing tobacco.

Good judgment comes from experience. Most experience comes from bad judgment.

Never miss a chance to keep your mouth shut.

Always drink upstream from the swimmers.

Grandpa was so sloppy at the table that they put his food in a large wooden bowl and had him sit at a little table in the corner. Later Dad saw Junior making something out of wood, so Dad asked what he was making. He said, "I'm making a wooden bowl for you."

Heaven should have room service or I won't go.

Two missionaries were lost in the jungle at night. They heard ominous drums getting louder and louder.

One said to the other: "I don't like the sound of those drums."

A voice in the dark said: "He's not our regular drummer."

I was asked to write my own epitaph. I wrote:

HE TOLD THE TRUTH

WHILE HE WAS ALIVE

NOW HERE HE LIES

AND SAYS HE'S 105

HOLY MAGIC

For millions of years our forbears believed in all kinds of Occult and Magic stuff. So now we are born with a little spot in our brain that yearns for magic etc. That is probably why there is no place on earth where the people don't have some kind of religion or other occult beliefs that help them through the night. Like some one once said: "If there was no God we would invent one." It is part of our brain's makeup and will not go away. Atheists believe there is no God. Polytheists say that all Gods are good. Henotheists say: "I'll believe in your God if you'll believe in mine."

HOW BIG IS THE UNIVERSE?

The Hubbard Telescope did an awesome job for years, but now it is almost worn out. It, and computers, told us that there are 300 billion stars in the Milky Way, our own Galaxy, and that there were at least 30 billion Galaxies just like ours, maybe bigger, maybe smaller. That would make the total number of visible [to the Hubbard] stars at a 9 with 21 zeros after it. Our star, the Sun, has nine planets circling it, but only one has life on it, it seems. It is quite likely that all other stars have planets going around them, maybe with life. Should we guess one in a hundred? One in a hundred thousand? Let's be ultra conservative and make it one in a million has life like ours. SO, just take six zeros off that previous number and that would say that a number with 15 zeros is the number of planets with life like ours. Of course, some of those people(?) would be way behind us in evolution and some way ahead of us. And considering that these beings would go through the same process of development, they probably "got religion" along the way. Of course there's no way it would be similar to our types.

WOULD A GOD BE SUBJECT TO THE LAWS OF PHYSICS AND MATH?

CHAPTER 35 - MARTIN LUTHER

Martin Luther, born 1483, died 1546, knew he was a bit famous but had no idea that there would be a holiday in his name. Luther, a Reformation leader, would be known for his questioning of long held rigid religious rules. His crusade would be initiated by the increasing abuses of the church.

After Luther, many found that literal reading of the Bible was alien to the text and that human imperfections were natural.

THE CAESARS

Our months called September, October, November, and December are Latin for ninth, tenth, eleventh and, twelfth. The numbers don't fit the months because Julius Caesar thought it would be nice to have a month named after him. He always got his way so that's how we got July. Then when Caesar Augustus came along, he did the same thing and that's how we got August.

Caesar was so brilliant and loved; his army would do anything he asked.

He was such a historical genius that later, German and Russian kings dubbed themselves Caesars. The Germans spelled it KAISER and the Russians spelled it TSAR. It is doubtful if any of these impersonators could make a decent Caesar Salad.

TAX CUTS

Tax cuts certainly improve the economy of those who get them.

Note: Don't tell the Riff-Raff about the cuts and refunds.

PILL PUSHERS

I just told my HMO Sawbones that most medical doctors wouldn't last a week in an Engineering Office because Engineers are not allowed to guess.

He didn't reply because he had just prescribed the wrong pills.

CHAPTER 36 - HOW CAN AN AIRPLANE FLY?

A long time ago, someone (Bernoulli) found out that the air pressure multiplied by the air velocity was always a constant. PV = C. The cross section of a wing is called an "airfoil." These are sort of curved on the top side and mostly flat on the bottom. So, the air passing over the top of the wing has to travel farther and it has to speed up to cover the same distance in the same time.

And, since P x C, then if V [velocity] is increased, P [air pressure] must be decreased. Well! If there is less air pressure on the top of the wing than there is on the bottom, the wing will be "sucked" upwards. The airplane knows this, aerodynamicists know this, so as the plane speeds down the runway, it will take off and fly.

That wasn't so hard was it? The next time grandma asks how that 200 ton thing stays up in the air, just tell her that P x V = C. It's not a miracle.

Miracles are things that happen but are not understood by the observer. If someone understands the event, it is commonplace. Ergo, planes fly.

CHAPTER 37 - HIGH ON AIRPLANES

As a lad on the farm I was in love with airplanes, and when I was about eight years old, my older brother, Lloyd, shouted at me that there was an airplane landing in our neighbor's pasture. It made my summer. It was about a mile and a half away but we ran all the way to see this homemade biplane sitting in the neighbor's cow pasture. It was REAL and we could feel it.

Later, while I was a student at Davenport High School, I had another brush with aviation. An old guy named B. J. Palmer had invented the artistry of Chiropractic and had built a school there to teach its wonders. Every summer they had a convention for their alumni with various festivities. My older sister, Goldie, was dating one of the students and had inside info. I found out that they were giving the conventioneers and their families FREE airplane rides at Cram Field nearby. [This airfield has since been housed-over.] I got in line with the families and was taken for somebody's kid and got my three minute ride. It was a tired Stinson Detroiter that only had one working brake. Who cares? Due to the large waiting crowd, the minute we took off on the grass field, the pilot made a steep turn to make a landing, followed by the unloading and reloading of the next in line.

The thing that stuck in my memory of that short heavenly ride was the noise. Instead of being wafted skyward in the arms of angels, it was more like sitting on a tractor engine at full throttle.

My second encounter with the heroics of aero-space was when a guy named Ben Gregory came to town in his all metal Ford Trimotor. He advertised rides over town at the price of a penny a pound. I weighed about a hundred pounds so bullied and threatened the whole family until I had accumulated a dollar. The evening of his arrival, Mr. Gregory flew over town at about 300 feet to advertise his enterprise. He had rigged up some spotlights out on the wing struts that shone back on the fuselage and at the same time he set off smoke pots. This made the airplane look like it was on fire and doomed. Our fire engine and men chased it around town until they felt foolish and realized it was a stunt. At the airport the next day I was weighed and relieved of my buck. When I went to board the plane, it was so full [twelve seats?] that the pilot, Ben himself, asked me to sit up by him in the copilot's seat.

WOW! This was the thrill of the year, maybe a ten minute ride, over town, the Mississippi River, and the Government Dam. I walked on air for a week.

Those old planes were pretty slow. They did not fly at the speed of sound.

They flew at the speed of smell.

CHAPTER 38 - MILKING METAPHORS

Most nice people understand the value of metaphorical stories and the life lessons that they lay out for your delight. Most of us understand the connotation when we tell about a religious figure being born of a lotus blossom and another of a virgin. And the physics of buoyancy do not allow walking on water no matter how nimble. Any botanist can discuss your chances of being reincarnated as a carnation or a crown prince.

These morality lessons are all GOOD; the problems start when we forget they are just metaphors.

PAGANS

Pagans are not "unbelievers" or "infidels." In Latin Paganus means "country people." Is that a bad name? In the old days people who lived in a village were called "villains."

THE GREEN GENESIS

A book by this name cited data that showed that if an wild animal was tamed for a pet, and if this went on for thousands of years, the young animals would eventually be born with the trait, talent, or tendency to be born amenable to be being a pet. The period required to make this revision in their natures seemed to run from ten to twenty thousand years.

This might explain such old cliché's as "dumb as an ox" or "sly as a fox" or "wise as an owl" or "smart as" whatever. Every species has honed its talent for survival or it would be extinct, or dead as a Dodo.

Maybe the reason Eskimos are not very interested in operas or crop rotation or ice sculpture is that they are too busy trying to survive. People native to the tropics see no need for building granaries and canning food for the next season. But if the earth's poles should slowly begin to shift, again, they would have a few thousand years to learn what the present dwellers of the so-called temperate zone had to learn. Like the squirrel said, "Save your nuts for the winter."

CHAPTER 39 - SKINNY DIPPING

Just think, around the year 2050, they will show comic documentaries about swim suits and how they grew smaller and smaller in the past and then disappeared when some diet guru came up with the idea that skinny dipping would make you skinny. Fat people will stop eating until they can skinny-dip with confidence.

CORSETS

Someone once said, "A lady is a woman whose whole spine touches the back of the chair." That is an interesting observation, but it could be conjectured that in a CORSET there is no other way to sit.

JFK wore one.

TROOPS

Our Army and Marines have a shortage of troops needed to handle our global obligations. BUT we have 870 GENERALS. No shortage there.

CATS

Cats are a waste of fur. And stupid. Even when it is 90 degrees outside, they still walk around in a fur coat.

BOTTLED

Farrah Fawcett is going to sell her own line of bottled water. At $5.00 a quart, it will be called "Fawcett Water."

NEW YORK

"Where ya from?"

"New York."

"I'm sorry."

"New York."

"I heard you; I just wanted to say I'm sorry."

DNA

In 50 years crime investigators will be able to detect DNA from the breath left by anyone at the crime scene in the last week.

CHAPTER 40 - PEOPLE WHO PRAY

If we didn't have that little spot in our brains that thirsts for the occult, we might be laughing at people on their knees praying to an invisible old guy in the sky who always needs money.

But no one should dismiss the religions of the world. Although some will cite the sins of the church in the past, the GREATER GOOD is in the results of meditation evoked by man's many rites and rituals. The relaxed mental and physical condition provided by contemplation and meditation are medicines that rejuvenate us and help us withstand the rigors of life.

REMEMBER: Abject poverty is the normal state of man. But we can all afford to help the poor who "are always with us." The benevolence of charity can provide a brain balm or sedative for us sinners.

All preachers predict that it's possible that people's pride will be piqued by the prospect of our pairing up with the philanthropists who provide pants and provender to poor impoverished people.

CHAPTER 41 - CIVILIZATION

Civilization and Christianity are marvelous ideas that have never been tried.

The main mysteries in Christianity are chocolate rabbits and colored rabbit eggs.

The invention of the idea of HEAVEN gave HOPE to everyone in a miserable state.

Someone once said that if you had an infinite number of monkeys sitting at typewriters, they would eventually type out the complete works of Shakespeare. Whoever said that did not specify the ground rules. First, if every letter that was correct was saved, then one sentence would only take a few hours to be correctly done. But if nothing was saved until the whole works was complete, then it would take an infinite number of years. Someone once calculated that if you took a simple ten word sentence, a computer could accidentally repeat such a sentence, if it saved the good letters, in about two days. But if it had to get the whole thing right, then it would take millions of years. So if that's the way it goes, the stupid problem is greater than monkeys and even computers.

Everyone seems to have split personalities. One side of my brain I display to others and one side that I keep hidden.

This should scare you.

CHAPTER 42 - SOLUTIONS

Many of our problems were solved years ago in other countries but our country is so big and important that we can't copy the little guy.

For example, in a lot of places the loser in a law suit pays the expenses of the winner. This sorts out silly suits. But our American Bar Association would scream and have a tizzy.

Immigrants are another example. Many European countries have to import cheap foreign labor, BUT, they know who they are and where they are because those countries require everyone to carry an identity card that is hard to forge. They are just as democratic as we are, but their police always ask for that card first. Here, our police aren't even allowed to ask if a bad guy on the street is a border jumper.

Some strange guys take flying lessons and bump into buildings.

Me: "Can I buy you a drink?"

She: "Why you're old enough to be my father."

Me: "Could be. What was your mother's name?"

CHAPTER 43 - COMMENTS

If you don't want gays to get married, make it mandatory.

What do they mean by 'freedom of the press?" A two inch ad costs $250.

Royalty cannot work unless all parties Involved agree to play "pretend."

To hide your laughter concerning someone, tell them a joke.

If your bride tells you she's a hooker, advise her to keep her head down when she hits the ball.

Nude pictures of ugly women are hard to "come" by.

SECRETS

We have many laws designed to keep secret things that are illegal, immoral, or just a little dishonest. Samples:

a. You cannot inquire as to a job applicant's age, religion, race, color, ethnic background, sexual orientation, or previous condition of servitude.
b. Income tax returns are secret. If these data were public we could double the nation's income.

c. A wife can't testify about what her husband told her about his crime. Why NOT?
d. A confession of a crime must follow certain procedures. Why? The murderer didn't follow any procedures, did he?
e. A defense attorney cannot reveal the guilt of his client. So if there was a second shooter on the "grassy knoll," and he tells his lawyer, that guy must take the secret to his grave. What about the GREATER good?
f. The law protects a reporter from revealing his sources. Lately reporters have been making up shit, because it's EASIER.
g. Anybody can use any name he wants here, but, not in other countries.
h. If union management couldn't hide what they do with the dues , membership would increase a LOT.
i. If everyone's finger prints and DNA were kept in a big computer data bank, think of all the taxes we could save.
j. Some countries have full, public, gun registration. And they don't have our problems any more.
k. In the sale of airliners, all customers have a right to know what other guys paid for their airplanes. Why can't we have that system for pills and pharmaceuticals? It would be fairer.
l. Malpractice actions in court should be made public.
m. Frivolous lawsuits should be made public to protect us from the people who make a living that way.
n. We could go on and on....

CHAPTER 44 - DREAMS

Life is but a dream—to most—but if it's a dream, remember it is all in your HEAD

Why are some races more muscular than others? Maybe it depends on who came out of the woods (jungle?) last.

You shouldn't judge a man by the color of his neck.

Judging a book by its cover is an art that takes a while to accomplish. Once you get it down, it is a big help in judging people

Like erections, elections have no conscience.

THOUGHTS

If you are applying for a job, put some of you favorite perfume or aftershave on your resume. It wooden hoit!

If you visit someone in a hospital, it's a good place to take flowers. Hospitals have lots of flowers.

If you visit an art gallery or museum, you should take pictures. They have more than enough.

If you are invited to a family picnic, be sure to bring some aunts.

The early bird may get worms but the second mouse gets the cheese.

Reporter: "Are you religious?"

Lady: "Yes, and I have a photograph of Jesus right over my bed."

Reporter: "I can probably get you a million for the negative."

Photo Op Award: The President waving at Stevie Wonder.

If I gauge Nixon, Reagan and George W. as average caliber thinkers and you think they aren't brilliant, what does that say about you and me and our standards?

I am a member of the National Responsibility Party. I am the only member.

Not everyone is born with good hand / eye coordination. When I rode horses as a boy, I always had to hang on to the horse's mane because I had no seat, and no saddle. Some things do not require two-hand coordination. The flute, saxophone, harmonica, ocarina, etc are played one note at a time. If you play a piano with one hand, no one wants to listen. Shooting a gun at a still target requires only limited coordination and some patience. Pitching a baseball should be easier than batting. One hand versus two. Maybe.

No atheist ever killed anyone in the name of a Deity.

Some day our government will get so complicated that the Cabinet will have to be maybe 25 or 50 Vice Presidents with designated power to run their departments.

All religions are good for the people. It's the magic stuff in the dogmas that causes the doubts.

CHAPTER 45 - THE END IS COMING

Whether you're into numismatics or gerontology, or if you are an actuarial number cruncher, chances are you will be dead in the next ten decades.

She was more fun before she became a virgin.

THE WRONG SEX

What if God or nature put a person in a body with the wrong plumbing? The brain of one sex in the body of another? Then that person would be sexually attracted to a brain of the opposite sex, right? So what's the problem?

Marriage is not a RIGHT but it is a RITE invented by people. This rite can be amended by people whenever the current customs change.

CHAPTER 46 - SOMEONE SAID...

Someone said that average people think that Reagan and the Bushes are brilliant, while brilliant people think they are average. Note: An average I.Q. is 100.

"You can't fool the American voters" HAH!

Examples of the barely qualified:

NIXON ran for office so often he became a well known name. He was probably smarter than AVERAGE voters.

REAGAN was handsome so all the women voted for him. Like Nixon, he had graduated from a small college so he must have been better educated than most. In his speeches he read whatever they wrote for him.

GEORGE THE LESSER had a pile of money to spend, but still did not win the popular vote the first time around. The Republican biased Supreme Court had to appoint him

"Gay" people deserve the same rights as "straight" people. By the accident of birth, we could be born either way.

The marriage ritual was invented by men and women and has been revised many times. With the advent of agriculture came property rights, then ownership of one or more women, then rights were formalized with rites called marriage. Eventually it included the benefits in taxes, insurance, pensions, Inheritance, and even visitation rights.

A family life is a good life. We should encourage all families, whatever kind.

A POPE

John Paul II said that atheism is the root of all evil. Good for him. Just think; if we could abolish atheism then Jews would stop killing Arabs and Arabs would stop killing Jews, and Shiites would stop killing Sunnis and visa versa. And Iraq then would make no more bombs. KILL the atheists!

CHARITABLE CONTRIBUTIONS

With computer sciences expanding exponentially, soon religious organizations will be told of all the contributions made to them according to that which is listed on our tax forms. Then they can BILL the phony donors and they will be swamped with money.

TRAVEL INSURANCE

A while back there were machines in airports that would issue you a policy on the spot, some as low as one dollar for $8,000 flight insurance. I knew a bachelor who spent four dollars, bought four policies and mailed them to four different ladies with each listed as his beneficiary. He said he didn't crash but all the policies paid off.

COUNTRY MUSIC

If you suffer from depression, try this old trick. You play a country song backwards. Then you get out of jail, your dog gets better and your wife comes home.

SPEED

"Everything is comparative," said the snail, as he watched the turtle whizzing by.

WASPS

I once had four uncles, Bill, Ott, Henry, and Walter who, like most others in the agricultural Midwest, assumed they were WASPS (White Anglo Saxon Protestants) even though they had never attended a church. When my sister, Honey, married a Catholic they were all invited to the wedding and showed up on time. During the Catholic ceremony they all four dutifully stood on the front steps of the church. They wouldn't dare go inside; they were Protestants, very sure in their status in life. They would not have thought of themselves as biased, just cautious.

NUDISM

Nudism was natural before they invented clothes. It has been around for maybe five million years. So, nudism has been around longer than "clothism."

Don't quote me. Anon.

CHAPTER 47 - COMMENTARY

People who eat a lot of licorice are often anise retentive.

In German, the slang word for this stuff is "Bear Shit."

My Pekinese dog is not fat, she's just big boned.

We should require expensive licenses for KILLER dogs.

If you don't ask questions about religious MAGIC you're a Holy fool.

The Catholic Church has made thousands of so called Saints. Jesus has been dead for 2000 years. Isn't it time they made him a Saint?

The terrorists think it's okay to murder people in tall towers, but it's a sin to wear nice dresses.

The Shiites hate electric gadgets such as electric fans. We've all heard about the Shiites hitting the fan.

High fevers, like I had with the mumps when I was a boy, caused my vision to narrow down so that I thought I was looking through a tunnel, and also, once I felt like I was floating around the ceiling looking down at myself. My old Doc explained that this often occurs during a high fever. He would have laughed if I had called it a "near death" experience. It was only the MUMPS.

If you can survive a high dive from an altitude of about 600 feet, you would be reaching your terminal velocity, and so, you could also survive a dive of 10,000 feet. Try it. Let me know.

Is your future past?

They always say peaceful ways are the best. Write a letter to your government, that's the American way. Hah.

I wrote to our leaders about:

A possible attack

An unbreakable secret code

An easy way to make hydrogen

An easy way to double deck our freeways

So far I've been waiting two years for some reply. I even addressed the letters to the correct office door number of the Head of the CIA, Homeland Defense, Head of the Senate Intelligence Committee, Secretary of State, and Secretary of Defense. Maybe the mail is slow.

Vegetarians are incomplete. They are missing many needed nutrients. Our insides are similar to that of bears, monkeys and pigs. We are omnivores. And, the smartest animals are us and the carnivores. Elephants and horses can learn stuff by rote, but don't seem to learn anything for themselves. By the way, when you pull a carrot out of the ground, did you ever listen to its faint scream?

There have been many good stories and movies about the start of Christianity and how its messages are models to live by, especially the New Testament. The Old Testament is full of crap and folk lore that insult the intellect. There's not enough water on earth to flood all the land, for instance, and by the way, why do artists always draw Noah's Ark with pointy ends? It wasn't going anywhere.

I wish some one would research and write about the committee, conclave, or whatever it was called, around the second century A.D. that got together to decide which of the existing stories to put together into a New Testament. The dozens of stories they rejected are now called The Apocrypha, which sort of means that maybe they are just legends and not true enough to go into the new good book. Some of my writings would come under that classification, I suppose. Most of the rejected stories were in Greek, maybe they had trouble, "lost in translation." If there are any records of this important group, it would certainly be interesting to read about their travails.

I'll bet $100 that in fifty years, school children will be taught by Brain Experience Transfer. Then they won't have to study all those books and if all the book larnin' is slipped into their heads by a computer helmet, they would have lots of time to do research and expand their intellect by other new means. Maybe cure cancer or even the common cold.

My old man used to say that a lot of rich people didn't know how to spend their money. He thought that the first thing they should do is improve themselves. Also, he said that most snobs didn't know how to put it on (pull it off). Which reminds me that the first time I put on a full dress suit, my dog tried to bite me. I guess that's what I got for trying to put on the dog.

She: "Do men ever cry during sex?"

He: "I did once."

She: "Why?"

He: "I don't know, maybe it was that damn pepper spray."

114

All wars are bad, but Viet Nam was no worse than the rest of them. The Communists declared that they would take over the world and after WW II they were occupying maybe a dozen countries in Europe. Germany, Korea and Viet Nam were divided in half, half commie, half free, so the commies made a move on each of them. President Truman stopped them in Berlin and Korea, and when the reds spent millions of lives and a lot of their resources for four or five years in Viet Nam, they gave up their expansive and expensive ideas. Because of Nam, the threat of Communism is no longer a problem.

Castration was used at times on rapists and sex offenders. Maybe they have a strong lobby.

You can't sin if you don't believe in sin. So if you do not believe in Hell, you can't go there.

Many of the problems of today were solved long ago in other countries, but the U.S. is so big and important that we can't copy the little guy.

If Hollywood is so eager to make money, how come nepotism is so prevalent? Wouldn't it make more sense to hire the most talented instead of friends and relatives? But, maybe they get kick backs—who knows what evil lurks in the hearts of men—the Shadow, he do.

CHAPTER 48 - RELIGION SOMETIMES GETS IN THE WAY OF MORALITY

Religion sometimes gets in the way of morality.

Examples: The Inquisition. Pedophile Priests.

When did our kids take the tunes out of music?   A cannon or drum barrage is not music.

ELLEN

Ellen Degeneres said: "They say we only use 10% of our brains. Wouldn't it be great if we learned to use the other 60%?"

When I was young, the guys always tried to "feel up" their dates. But, today, everything is digital.

HOLLYWOOD

A would-be actor met a producer at a party and asked, "Can I send you my resume?"

Producer: "I'm looking for a guy like you. Come in at 6 A.M."

Would-be: "What does it pay/"

Producer: "Nothing."

Would-be: "Okay."

Nudie bars don't interest me. When you've seen one naked woman, you want to see them all.

THE NOTRE DAME CATHEDRAL

This is where a Gargoyle is a spittin' image.

NOTE: Gargoyle = gargle-er.

TAXES

We could get out of debt if we put a 10% sales tax on anything with a price ending in 99.

COLLEGES

Some times when you ask a business associate what school he attended he will mention a place no one has ever heard of: like Tumor Tech. When this happens, be diplomatic and ask: "What's the matter with your football team?"

Every time I ask this, they answer, "Oh, we're rebuilding."

WALL STREET TIP

Zeppelin travel is way down.

Big bosoms become a beacon (P.T. Barnum: A sucker is born every minute)

GEATEST DOCTOR

He said, "Your guess is as good as mine."

We hear tell from the Alaska Fish and Game Dept. as follows:

Both male and female reindeer grow antlers in the summer each year, but the males drop theirs at the beginning of winter. Female reindeer retain theirs until they give birth in the spring.

So if Santa wants reindeer with antlers he has to use GIRLS.

Makes sense, only females would be able to drag a fat-ass old man in a red velvet suit all over the world in one night and not get lost.

CHAPTER 49 - ALASKA

When Alaska became a state, congress discussed whether or not to make it into TWO states. But Texas objected because then they would have been the THIRD largest state.

My favorite opera composer is JOE GREEN

(Giuseppi Fortunio Franceco Verdi)

The Fundamentalist Fanatics, FFERS, probably haven't thought it through any more than any other M-Fers.

Mother who always say, "Always clean your plate!" are making kids eat more than they want and more than they should. My mother said that the upper class always left a little on their plates as a sign of their respect for their bodies. A clod will wipe up his plate with a piece of bread to show how good it was, and in some societies a loud belch will signify a compliment to the chef. As our nation of plenty grows more and more obese, airlines have to widen the seats and soon will have to weigh each passenger and make sure the craft is balanced, fore and aft.How the hungry Haitians hate us!

"My Chee-wah-wah isn't fat, he's just big boned"

Some one should start the Concentration Camp Diet. You get nothing but cabbage leaf soup for two years. You will get down to one hundred pounds, regardless of your "glands" or big bones.

There once was a Polka called, "I don't want her you can have her, she's too fat for me." If you danced to that for an hour, you lost five pounds, and probably some fat friends.

When I was in college, the biggest guy on our football team, weighed 270 pounds. We thought, "What a blimp!" Today, he might be too small to make the team.

DON'T WASTE YOUR MONEY ON CON MEN (Or women)

If they say they can give you a message from your dearly departed (dead relatives) they are lying. Just because you can't see the trick doesn't make it a miracle. Accept that you family or others who have passed away are gone for good and they cannot speak from the grave. If they could, the cemeteries would be noisy places. And if there was a spirit world, they would talk to you every day, probably telling you of everything you are doing wrong.

To explain the TV shows and such where the guy or gal tells you things that only you should know, let me start by explaining something. Mind reading has been possible for some people for ages. When it is firmly and scientifically demonstrated, it isn't always 100 percent accurate and nobody gives a damn so there isn't really any money in it. But now, if I told you to think of your dead Dad so I could contact him, Presto! It worked. In a picture in your mind you see him in his favorite red shirt.

I, the con man, will say, "I see him wearing his favorite red shirt." Wow, now you'll believe anything.

CHAPTER 50 - POLLUTION

Maybe it is a Gawd that is polluting our world. Someone is making our volcanoes spew lava into the sea, making tornados and tidal waves to despoil our cities and making our stars blow up. Maybe the so-called global warming is just a warning about the next ice age that's bound to come. They do come in cycles, called ice cycles. When they hang from the eaves too long we are on the eave of another ice cycle.

MANUFACTURING OVERSEAS

We need a law that says "Companies that have their products made overseas must pay a minimum wage per U.S. standards." But how could you get that through a congress that depends upon these companies for reelection money!

WHAT IS A MOOSE?

My dictionary says: It is the largest of the American Elk. Try telling that to the Moose lodge. Or the Elks lodge. But they're all Goodfellows, or Woodmen. The Masons would be mortarfied.

GAYETY

Non-religious studies find that people do not get to choose their sexual orientation (gaiety?) ,they are born with it. So why should we screw them over about it. Almost no men would choose the life in the queer society, as it has hundreds of drawbacks and discrimination problems. I knew a little baby of two years who ran like a girl and when he was four he asked his mother if he could wear dresses. These are cases where one department of nature makes the body with certain plumbing and another department makes the brain with different wiring. Like the eyeballs, the design is perfect but the manufacturing is weak on quality control.

Note: In a medical study of young future farmers of America, only one kid in a thousand had really perfect vision. The vast majority were 'good enough' but not perfect.

Note: Today, it's hard to find one man who wants to get married, let alone two. So why would two men want to get married to each other?

WHAT IS A JEW?

On our way home from Lutheran Preschool, my little son asked, "What's a Jew?" I replied, "Well, Jesus was a Jew." My son declared, "Yeah, but he's a Lutheran now!"

My question: If Jesus were alive today, what would he say about the Israelis?

My answer: If Jesus were alive today he would be so old that his opinion wouldn't amount to much.

WHAT'S AN UMLAUT?

If your baby is born with two freckles on the top of his head, you should name him "UMLAUT."

THE TOP SECRET

Our government now has a Top Secret Cabinet Post. It is in charge of "Making Up Shit."

FAIR TRADE

Free trade = bad

Fair trade=good

All countries want to sell us their goods but when it comes to buying ours they think up devious ways to resist. We have pacts with other countries that allow an import tax on things such as autos and auto parts but truck parts were omitted. So certain Asians who shall remain nameless (Japan) assemble their autos here from parts and assemblies that come in containers marked "truck parts." No tax!

BUY AMERICAN

That was our slogan during the Great Depression. A Japanese Engineer told me (his name was Tscada) that he would rather buy an American car but his neighbors would shun him. They are so patriotic, they want to be loyal to their factories. We are allowed to sell our cars there, but only after a complete inspection of each car to "see if it is safe." This is an act that disassembles the car and costs thousands of dollars, which must be added to the selling price. That's patriotic. That's Free Trade but not Fair Trade

So, an American car costs an extra $20,000 in Japan, yet their cars sell for less here than in Japan. You figger.

Years ago, Japan openly boasted that they would take over all auto sales in the U.S. So far, at least in California, they are half way there. When I asked a General Motors Public Relations man why they did not start a "Buy American" campaign, he replied, "We are major stock holders in all Japanese auto makers; we make money no matter where you buy." Patriotic?

RETRIBUTION

When the elder Bush was elected he heard about the Asian tricks and he decided to get an even playing field, at once! His advisors were against it. They noted that under Reagan, the

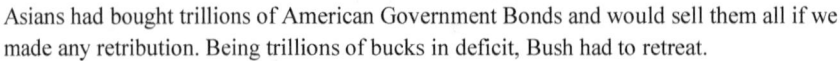

Asians had bought trillions of American Government Bonds and would sell them all if we made any retribution. Being trillions of bucks in deficit, Bush had to retreat.

PROGRESS

Some old fuddy duddies think Progress is dangerous, to be resisted at all costs. Progress eventually proves old fuddy duddies WRONG!

FIRM BELIEFS

Once, browsing thru a library, I found a book called, "The Majority is Aways Wrong." It cited hundreds of examples. One such firm belief is the one mothers tell their daughters: "Don't let the boys see your underpants!"

FREE TRIP TO HAWAII

I've found through personal accidental experience that the company offering such a prize already has a relative of the owner who is designated to win it.

A few years back, an auto dealer sent car door keys in the mail to thousands of suckers, potential buyers. If your key fit the door lock in a certain car in their show room, the car was yours. One little old lady tried her key and it worked. The dealer said he was sorry but that she was not the designated winner. Naturally she raised quite a fuss. Finally, they offered her a nice used car and she accepted. The story made the news on page 34, no one was too surprised.

Fifty years ago, my neighbor was in charge of a "giveaway" of a list of prizes and told me the top prize was a thirty inch television which he would win, and I could win the five gallons of paint donated by one of his sponsors.

As Jimmy Durante used to say: "These are the exigencies that prevail."

ON STAGE

During the big war that was in all the papers, WW II, I was in uniform going through Hollywood. Jimmy Durante had a weekly radio show before a sold out live audience at the NBC studios at Sunset and Vine. I wanted to see him so someone took me backstage where I could watch from the wings. Great! At the end of the show, Durante was taking bows and coming off and going back and taking more bows. When he saw me, he grabbed my hand and took me out to take a bow with him. The people cheered. I had my five minutes of fame.

NEPOTISM

In Hong Kong, I once read an English news item about their Neptune Society. They had named Queen Elisabeth their Honorary Chairman of the "Nepotism" Society. This seemed apropos because when she is done she will leave her job to her son. Nepotism.

And since Hollywood is out to make money, lots of money, how come they don't hire the most talented people for actors, directors, assistant producers and screen writers? No, they hire their relatives. Think how much better the movies would be if they hired the BEST.

HEAVENLY LAWSUITS

Some day, in our litigious society, some one is going to sue a church, preferably one with lots of money. They will state that the church promised them that their loved one was assured that he or she was destined for heaven and that he or she never arrived there. They will mention a pact between the dearly departed and the survivors. He/she was to let them know when they had arrived. No such message had been received and therefore the church had made a false promise, and maybe had profited from the dirty deal. Some day, it will happen. If I get there I'll ask them why they didn't call like they promised.

CHAPTER 51 - FUN FROM FRACTURED FRENCH

We use a lot of French in our language and the way we use it is sometimes fun or funny.

When we eat out, in a restaurant, we often talk about the Maitre D. This is short for Master of the Hotel. We're probably not in a hotel. Hello.

Everybody uses the term "Gourmet." There are Gourmet Eateries, Gourmet Chinese food etc. In Paris, I looked it up in a French dictionary. It said: "A wine taster." And a gourmand is a "glutton" So next time I have a gourmet hot dog, I'll know it is a wine taster hot dog.

Jeanne d'Arc, the ancient fighter lady who talked to God, has a name pronounced "John Dark." This does not mean that the light is out in the bathroom.

Everyone has probably received an invite with R.S.V.P. on the bottom...We know it means "let us know if you're coming." The translation is "Repondez s'il vous plait." I know there should be an accent circumflex like a ^ over the A in the word plait, but my keyboard refuses to do it. Literally it means "Respond if it you please." It is being nice in Nice.

Have an hors d'oeuvre [or durve]. My French dictionary has several meanings: "Outwork, digression, side dish, dainties." Take your pick. Some RUDE men say it means whores ovaries, but there has never been a valid basis for this belief. "Have a dainty.. Some taste like chopped rubber bands on a cracker.

To my French friends; Jean, Gerard, Veronique, Gisselle, I apologize, don't write nasty letters.

Speaking of things French, Champagne was supposed to have been invented by an old Monk named Dom Perignon. If you ask anyone under thirty, "What's the BEST champagne?" they will probably say "Dom Perignon," even though they have never tasted it. it's about $75 a bottle in a store and much more in a restaurant. This is called MARKETING. You never see their ads or commercials. But if a Prop Man in movies or TV can arrange for it to be called "the best" somewhere on a show, he can get wealthier overnight.

Every year in Paris they have a blind taste test for all the leading champagnes to pick the Top Ten. Dom Perignon has never won although many that sell for around $30 are included. Like Bollinger, Taitenger, Mumms, Perrier, Piper Heidsieick, Cliquot Veuve and others. *A votre sante*.

France won lots of wars under Napoleon the Corsican, but since then, well there's 1870, 1918, 1940? They're lovers.

Anyone jumping off a bridge in Paris will be in Seine.

THE MIGHTY BRITISH EMPIRE

On which the sun never used to set. At that time a British schoolboy would be hard pressed to name every British colony around the world. Britannia ruled the waves. This MIGHTY empire was made possible by their discovery that many, many nice civilized rich countries around the world did not have GUNS. Their excuse for this aggression was that they were bringing civilization to them.

The Rajahs and people of India, for instance, were parading elephants covered with precious stones down their parade routes while the English were still living in their forests, maybe in the trees. Bring us your civilization, please, take our riches, please. What are "guns?"

Now, who else can I insult?

Oh, yes, the Germans and the Italians.

THE GERMANS

In this century, the Germans were very good at winning the first half of wars, like WW I [that was not it's name at the time] and WW II. Germany won a war against France around 1870. Although the French had more soldiers, the Krupp family had just invented long range cannons with barrels made of steel. Some French soldiers complained that thy never even got to fire a shot.

The French also had more soldiers when Hitler sent some of his army down into the Rhineland to occupy it before WW II. Hitler wanted to know how the French would react. They did nothing, so he was encouraged.

THE ITALIANS

Supposedly, Marco Polo brought pasta back from China and it became a staple of the Italian diet. Then after Columbus came to America, eventually tomatoes were introduced into Europe. And the Italians made tomato sauce to put on the pasta. The question is what did Italians eat before all this? No spaghetti?

Archeologists have been digging up thousands of old skeletons from the many battles between the Romans and the Germanic Tribes 2000 years ago. The Romans called the Germans "barbarians" because they thought the German language was just a lot of mumbling. From the thousands of bones, they came to the conclusion that the average Roman soldier was five foot one inches tall and the Germans were five foot eight.

When the northern Germans decided to migrate for better farm land and climate, they took their time, stopping to raise crops and children along the way. When the Romans went to stop their advance, it was the first defeat for the famed Roman army. The Germans just kept coming, settled in southern France, then Spain and many continued to North Africa.

COWBOYS

Two Texas ranchers were getting drunk in a bar and arguing about who had the biggest ranch. One said, "My spread is so big that if I start out on side of the ranch in my car at sun-up, it will be sun-down before I get to the other side,"

The other said," Yeah, I used to have a car like that."

AN IMPORTANT GUY

A wife sent her husband to have his sperm tested for viability. When he returned, he was sporting a big cigar.

She said: "What did the Doctor say and why the big cigar?"

He replied: "The Doctor said that I was IMPOTENT!"

CHAPTER 52 - REPUBLICS

New republics produce democracy a little at a time. When ours started women could not vote or own property and were covered from chin to toe. And slavery was legal. The men who wrote "all men are created equal" really meant "all men are created the same way."

We have progressed so much that now we have more and more rights, for instance, whore houses are now required to have ramps for wheel chairs.

NEW COLLEGE COURSE

Bodice ripping for dummies

COACHES

A new NCAA rule specifies that any coach who announces that his team will "only play one game at a time" will have to play TWO games at a time until proven.

WILLS

Everyone should have a will. Unless your descendants can't read.

THE DEVIL YOU SAY!

If there were a devil he would think that God is evil.

SMOKE

Our tax dollars are being used to tell us that second hand smoke is bad for us. What about first hand smoke?

LIFE BEGINS AT FORTY

Translation: Our children are children until about the age of forty.

COLORS

If we changed the name of a color, what would it matter? Back in the caveman days, some one decided to call the color of cherries blue, others objected and a committee decided to call cherries red. Now you know.

CHAPTER 53 - COMFORTING THOUGHTS

It must be easy to learn to play the banjo, because you only have to learn one piece.

It must be fun to write country music, because you already have the tune.

ENGINEERING SCHOOL

On the day of the first lecture in Engineering College, the speaker usually tells you to take a good look at the student on your right and on your left. Because, a year from now, only one of you will still be here. "But be nice to those guys or gals because some day they could be your lawyer or your doctor."

HEART THROBS

There is no emotion in your heart, it is just a pump. But through the centuries, because we could feel the throbs of the heart, we have ascribed values and features to the heart that it does not have. It's just a pump.

If you say;

'You are heartless' it means 'you have no pump'

'My heart belongs to you' it means 'you own my pump'

'What's in your heart' it means 'besides blood'

'If I give my heart to you' it means 'I'll have no pump'

'It's a heart stopper' it means 'a pump malfunctions'

'My heart aches' it means 'another malfunction'

'In just a heartbeat' it means 'a portion of the pump action of the cardiovascular system that is a variable depending on the need for more or less blood during exercise or other excitation'. [Whatever]

Or

I've had a change of pump.

You are absolutely pumpless.

I left my pump in SFO.

The war hero was awarded the Purple Pump.

ABORTIONS

I believe abortions are good, especially retroactive.

PARDON MY MYTH

Myths, new or old, feed on insufficient information and a lack of evidence. This is sometimes called ignorance.

WAITER

"Waiter, take your thumb out of my soup!"

"I'm sorry but I have arthritis in my thumb and the hot soup reduces the pain somewhat."

"Well, take your thumb out of my soup and stick it up your ass!"

"Oh, I do that in the kitchen."

DROP OUTS

School dropouts make a conscious decision to remain uneducated for the rest of their lives.

REACH OUT AND SUE SOMEONE

We once belonged to a nice church in Sherman Oaks, California. It was a red brick building. Now, whenever I am filling out a form that asks: "Church preference," I always write: "Red Brick."

In this church, the housewives got together and decided to volunteer to take care of each other's small children and have a kind of Day Care place. No money was involved, they would use one of the Sunday School rooms when no one was using it during the week. Some of the mothers even got jobs.

After a couple of years, everything was still going smoothly but the mothers noticed that about half of the children seemed to be of another religion entirely. So they made a RULE; "Anyone using the Day Care facility had to be a member of THIS church."

WELL, some of the outsiders claimed that this was discrimination! And some threatened to SUE!

Maybe that's why some believe that we are a litigious nation. [L.A. has more lawyers than all of Japan]

HOW ABOUT THAT, SPORTS FANS?

I sent an idea to our newspaper but it was rejected. I suggested that between the Super Bowl and opening day for the baseball season, nothing much was happening so why not give everybody in the Sports Department time off to take a vacation? Any news on the minor sports could be carried in the Entertainment Section:

- Like the game where they throw stuff into the waste basket.
- Like the game where they have boxing and wrestling while wearing ice skates.
- Like the game invented for guys in hand cuffs, where they have to use their feet to move the ball.
- Or that other game where they practice beating nonexistent snakes and gophers with inadequate clubs, over bad terrain and in all kinds of weather.

WHITHER GOETH THE WHITES

Much of this country has been occupied by a couple of nations called Asia and Wetbackland. And this is supposed to be good for business. O.K. Then when the country is OVER 50% non-whites, our new lawmakers can vote to change the name to: The United Nations of America

A KING FOR US

Royalty are people you pay to be better than you. We could have royalty. Everyone interested could submit their resume and those experienced enough or otherwise eligible, would be entered in a lottery. The winner would be King [or Queen] and we would pay them to be better than us. YER MAJESTY !

CHAPTER 54 - NOTES

I am an experimental design and I get no respect...

She wore a black garter in memory of the guys who had gone beyond

Depression is curable; it's all in your head. Where else would it be?

I used to be egotistical but I got over it and now I'm the finest guy in town.

Ask any archeologist about the history of the earth, ask any astronomer about the history of the universe. Ask any anthropologist and they will tell you that superstition is bad luck.

There are thousands of rules in football and baseball and they confuse the "average" fan. Hence the popularity of basketball and soccer.

BRAND NAMES

Many brand names become so common in our usage that they become generic. Once when I bought a $250 Leica camera, my mother-in-law asked: "What kind of Kodak is that?"

When someone saw my hot-tub-spa they remarked: "That's a nice Jacuzzi." I had to explain that none of its parts were made by the Jacuzzi Company [which was out of business at the time].

SMOKING

Smoking is fun, therefore it must be a sin. Our Victorian mores about SIN are still with us. People who smoke after sex are getting two for the price of one.

CELEBRITIES

Never one to go out of my way to see a celebrity, never the less, after sixty years in Los Angeles, I can name a few I have run in to.

Eddie Rickenbacker, 1950, Pres. of Eastern Airlines, came to Lockheed.

Robert Gross,1948, Chairman, Lockheed, invited me to lunch.

Donald Douglas, Sr. and Jr.,1947, invited me to lunch.

Jimmie Doolittle, USAF General,1946, brief introduction.

Vera Miles and Anita Bryant, 1959 movie actresses, in small play with me.

Nile Kinnick,1941, Heisman Trophy Winner, State University of Iowa.

Tom Mix, 1936, cowboy star, brief intro.

Elmo Lincoln,1929, First Tarzan portrayer, visited our school.

Charlie Chaplin, 1972, Silent movie star. Took pic in Paris restaurant.

Jerry Colona, 1980, Comedian, met in Tail of the Cock restaurant.

Jack Benny, 1967, Comedian, he made fun of me in the lobby of movie.

Patricia Neal, 1965, brief introduction at friend's house.

Bob Hope and Les Brown, 1950, brief intro, Lockheed Airport.

Jimmy Durante, 1945, back stage, NBC Radio broadcast.

Nat King Cole, 1946, Piano player at Sonja Henie's birthday party.

Jack Carson, 1944, Radio Comedian, back stage, NBC broadcast.

Cletus Caldwell, 1962, made one Tarzan movie. Bombed.

During sales trips, met the following airline presidents and chief engineers:

Delta, Eastern, Braniff, Alaska, Aloha, Pacific Southwest, Canadian Pacific, Iberia, Olympic, El Al, North American, KLM, Air France, Mexicana, Aeronaves, Flying Tigers and Aeroflot.

Big deal.

CHAPTER 55 - BOTTLED WATER

When you travel to another country, buying bottled water is a good idea because their TAP water will be different than what you are used to. It will be something new to your guts. And their water may be no better or no worse than your own. Store-bought water costs more than milk or gasoline but we buy it because our tap water tastes like chlorine. You can get rid of that taste by running a bunch in a bucket and letting it set for a day or two. Then you will have water that is probably as good as anything you can buy. Most bottled water comes from the city's tap water, then it usually is filtered and later may have some minerals replaced for flavor.

Once when I was working as a laborer on the Missouri river banks with the U.S. Corps of Engineers, the foreman would hoist a barrel of brown water out of the brown river and try to settle the sediment by letting it set for a while. Each such barrel was given a thimble full of chlorine. This made it safe to drink, mud or no mud, and it was good.

The March, 2004, issue of Men's Health Magazine reviewed tests run on all the bottled water they could find. Chemically, they were all as clean as city water and they all tasted like water. Surprise! But they thought that carrying the bottles around made you look cool.

HAPPY MEDIUMS

People called Mediums are often seen on TV or elsewhere and the latest scam is to get you in touch with a dead relative – for a price. Some of these people can actually read minds, maybe 80% of the time. This has been proven with an abundance of tests but then one says, "So What?" Well, if you tell a gullible descendant that you can put them in touch with a dead relative, yippee! The mind reader expects you to picture grandma in your mind, and that's all he needs. He'll say, "She is wearing her favorite red dress." Well, that was just what you were picturing in your mind so he must be in touch with grandma. He's not talking to her, he's talking to you. End of story.

And if you believe in ghosts, your brain will let you see one, because that's what you want. Just remember, the ghost is in your head. It would take a supreme effort of Divine Intervention to scare up a real body of ectoplasm etc. just for your entertainment. Remember, without physical ears and sound sensors there is no sound. Without eyeballs and nerves to the brain there can be no sight. AND ALL SUCH MANIFESTATIONS REQUIRE FUEL. Nothing made of flesh and bones [and nerves] can operate without fuel. Our brains start to rot in a few minutes if not supplied with fresh blood. Every cell in our bodies requires blood on at least one side, constantly. I guess this means that all ghosts are deaf, dumb and blind, old European castles notwithstanding…

Everything that is TRUE should be able to be proven either in a scientific laboratory or in a court of law. So where's my soul, Dude?

THE IRAQI ARMY

In the Gulf War, most of the Iraqi army ran away and hid. It was a good idea for them. Big Bush said he couldn't send the troops on to Baghdad without the U.N.'s approval. Little Bush and Rummy decided they didn't need U.N. approval, and they could use a smaller army to get the job done. Once again, the Iraqi army ran away and hid, but after Bush declared victory, they came out of their hiding places long enough to kill a few Americans every day. They are not insurgents, they are the Iraqi army.

CHAPTER 56 - CONSERVATIVES

The famous E.L. Doctorow recently published a paper that was worth reading. He said that Conservatives are steered in all ways by the heads of the world's largest corporations and we are worse off now than in the McCarthy era. And a constant state of war is needed to do business and scare the voters. If this ongoing policy is not voided by some votes for sanity, no new meaningful elections will be held in the future.

Today we are a nation to be FEARED and this will spawn millions of new terrorists whose future goal will be to outdo each other.

Our reformation will depend on our own dissidents, as we sure as hell can't leave it to the politicians.

She: "You are an arrogant prick."

He: "Why should I suffer fools who reiterate the obvious?"

I could write a book....

There are certain times when it is perfectly proper to use the F--- word.

For example, the Captain of the Titanic said: "What the F—do you mean, we're sinking?"

And the Mayor of Hiroshima asked: "What the F--- was that?"

Amelia Earhart asked: "Where the F--- are we?"

CHAPTER 57 - MORE JOKES

If you don't want gays to get married, make it mandatory.

What do they mean by "freedom of the press?" A 2 inch ad costs $250.

Royalty cannot work unless all parties involved agree to play "pretend."

To hide your laughter concerning someone, tell them a joke.

If your bride tells you she's a hooker, advise her to keep her head down.

Nude pictures of ugly women are hard to come by.

CHAPTER 58 - LOCKING THE DOOR TOO LATE

When the 9/11 attacks were all over and the terrorist sponsors were celebrating, our government did all the things they should have done before. In an all out response to show how awake we now were we shut down the airlines and started getting interested in the passengers. Soon we formed the Home Security Department which was to combine all the sleeping giants into one big sleeping giant Nobody could believe that the terrorists were so dumb as to try the same trick twice, but that's the way we acted. Congress even rushed through a bill taking away a lot of the Civil Rights we were trying to hold up to the world as DEMOCRACY.

A lot of warnings were ignored simply because our government is so large that a warning is like a mosquito bite to a whale.

I once wrote a letter to a candidate telling him that his campaign was all wrong. I got a reply that said "Thank you for your support."

I once sent five letters to five departments warning of a type of attack that could easily be done, right now. I got NO answers. They must have high school kids opening letters for which they are paid by the amount opened.

My home town was so small that the population doubled every time a train went through.

DISSADENTS GALORE

Every government that is totalitarianistic has its share of dissidents. Russia, China, India, Iran, Iraq, North Korea and any other country that was ever under an occupying power. We've read stories and seen melodramatic movies about the brave partisans who risked their lives to harass and stymie the bad dictator or occupier but where are the tales about the anti-Nazi fighters of Germany.

The Germans keep very exact records of everything they have ever done and they admit that almost twelve million civilians were executed during WW II. If six million were Jews, were the other six million not worth mentioning?

Like ourselves, most Germans ignore the long term public interest for the short term private gain, especially when the quick fix gives instant gratification.

As it did here, the German metaphoric wall between church and state was gradually eroding. Nazi crimes were only obvious to those who witnessed them, as government press releases let everyone guess at what was happening. Those who resisted evil were executed. How many? Probably millions. Some day some one will add them up for a foot note for history scholars.

Today, any anti-Nazi protagonists might come across like any other of history's assiduous arrivists, eager for acceptance but swimming against a very old tide.

The pre-war Germans were themselves a part of a multi-cultured world that later collapsed from its own confrontations.

I predict, some day there will be a full accounting

CHAPTER 59 - WHO IS BUSH THE LESSER?

In the beginning he appeared to be very Algerish. But it soon became clear that he couldn't find his way out of a simple bureaucratic maze even with the aid of an alidade.

Future historians will study him as an example of agriology or alexia.

I must be kidding. Maybe.

It is easier to understand others than yourself.

If you think your cat really loves you, try leaving the door open.

We love all the parts of the occult and religion, especially the sci-fi parts and the magic acts.

MALPRACTICE INSURANCE

When I was twenty one, I asked a young lady if she would like to go horseback riding. She said she had never tried it but would sure like to try. So we drove out to a stable known to rent riding horses and announced our intentions. The wrangler in charge welcomed us but asked us to first sign a waiver against any injury claims. It sounded logical, so we signed. The ride and the date were uneventful.

I wondered many times why medical practitioners didn't use the same system. Just sign a waiver and then the Doc doesn't have to spend half his income on malpractice insurance, and he could lower his fees.

I asked my old family Doc about this and he said that the lawyers passed laws against it because they needed the income from malpractice suits. Well, we certainly wouldn't want our lawyer to starve, would we? We will need him to take over our estate when we pass on.

Before any surgery or "hands on procedure" we are asked to sign a dozen papers after they've taken away our glasses, but the lawyers say that NO waiver is good enough

TRAFFIC CONGESTION

It can only get worse. Will Rogers once said that there wouldn't be any traffic jams if only the cars that were paid for were allowed on the roads.

There are two ways to reduce the bumper to bumper business:

One: Put an upper deck on the busiest roads.

Two: Make the freeways into Toll Roads during the busiest hours on the busiest roads. A magnetic sticker for your windshield would identify you to the cameras which would catch and bill violators. A monthly, or longer, fee would pay your way. History shows how tolls reduce traffic. We'll have to do it some day; it is time to start designing it.

If an upper deck were added where needed, a driver could have a choice i.e. go on the old lower deck for free or, choose the upper deck where you drop a two dollar chip in a slot and get away from the crowds. This method would pay for itself even though the term "freeway" would become an oxymoron.

CHAPTER 60 - FAITH

It has been said that 99.9% of the people are of the same faith as their parents. This reinforces the old adage that you have to mold them while they are young [or they'll get moldy]. So I suppose they all attend their parents' church, temple, synagogue, shrine, gazebo, golden calf house or Minaret of the Almighty Dollar.

Nonbelievers stay home and watch the ball game.

MUSLIM FAITH

These people believe that the best government is one run by the mosque. They think democracy smells of Christianity. Out of twenty some Muslim countries, the majority have rejected democracy, they don't trust politicians.

Do we?

ON SPEAKING TERMS

There are probably people in the universe who are much more advanced than we are, and if there is a God, I believe that He would rather talk to those guys than to us..

DEE – VORSE

Fifty percent of marriages fail because 100%, oops 98% of the couples have one horny member. Isn't that a "strange piece" of news?

CHAPTER 61 - DEGRADATION

If a story starts with "back when Adam was a boy," you should automatically dichotomously degrade it.

AMERICAN ARISTOCRATS

IF America had aristocrats, New York would be the one place they would shun. IF we wanted aristocrats, we would naturally need a King for the Top Dog. Getting a King would be easy, we hold a lottery of those most qualified to be TOKEN leaders, the winner would be King, and we would pay him to be better than us.

On the other hand, we could approach The British Empire and explain that we're sorry about the revolution, and would they take us back into the "empire." Assuming they would, then we would get representation in Parliament according to our population and we would be the majority. SO we pass a law that the capitol of the "empire" be moved out of London and into Washington D.C. Then England could become the 51st state.

OUTSIZING, EXPORTING JOBS

Being a soldier overseas [like Iraq] is nasty work so maybe we should export such jobs. We could probably hire the whole Hindu Army of Calcutta for maybe $499 a year. The Hindus never did like the Muslims anyhow.

HOW TO MAKE AN H-BOMB

Dial our 900 number to get this info at only $2.99 a minute.

AIR CRASH SURVIVAL INSURANCE

Air travel is the safest mode BUT once in a great while there is a problem, such as fire and smoke in the cabin even though smoke is not permitted. They say that more crash victims die of smoke inhalation than from the sudden stop. So I designed a smoke mask from things I had around the house. Whenever you buy a new blanket, most come in a strong, clear plastic case with a zippered end. If you leave that end open and put the case over your head to rest on your shoulders you will still be able to see clearly and smoke will not enter because there is almost no airflow in or out. Your hands will still be free to do what they do and there will be enough air in the mask for about three minutes. This should give you enough time to exit the airplane unless of course you spend that much time fighting your fellow passengers while trying to get your office briefcase out of the upper storage bin, in which case you deserve to die.

I carry mine folded as flat as a road-kill-squirrel and keep it in my pants pocket which I hope will remain with me at all times. The zipper has never set off an alarm in the airport security search because they assume it's my pants zipper.

As an optional accessory, at extra cost, I carry two or three deflated toy balloons in my shirt pocket. In the event there is some warning about the approach of an untoward landing, you can blow up these balloons and when and if they are needed you can release this air supply into the bottom of your hood to replace the foul air or smoke therein.

You should know from experience that if you go to the trouble of using this precaution, you will never, never, never need it.

CHAPTER 62 - MADE IN CHINA

Most of the things in my house were made in Asia by fetuses paid seventeen cents a year. I'd rather buy American, but our manufacturers can have them made cheaper over there. Either that or the Asians ran our people out of business by selling at a loss until they had cornered the market.

MUSINGS

It's easy to get into Med. School. Just WILL them your body.

Anthropology is a science in which people study people. It takes four years.

Flabbergasted means you are appalled at your weight

Willy-Nilly means you are impotent.

If you walk with a lisp, it's a lymph.

Sometimes age brings wisdom, sometime it smarts.

Life begins at forty and that's when it begins to show.

A gargoyle is a spitting image.

WHAT ARE THE ODDS

Shouldn't betting on heads or tails be a 50-50 proposition? If a casino had a daily game where people could bet heads or tails to double their money, they could call it "Minority Wins." At the end of the day, the smaller group, heads bettors or tails bettors would be paid double of whatever they bet. Minority Wins. The majority would be the losers and the casino would keep the difference. So the house would always make a profit except in the rare case of a tie. How come the house always wins when everyone has a 50-50 chance?

CHAPTER 63 - HOW TO SMOKE

No one recommends smoking except the tobacco companies. HOWEVER, if you must smoke, or are thinking about starting—that sounds SO stupid, no one seriously considers the pros and cons of smoking. Some time in Junior High or Elementary School, you just can't wait to try a cigarette. After smoking for sixty years without a lung problem, But I have recently quit merely because of my age.

No, I wasn't trying to get another five years in a nursing home.

No, I wasn't trying to protect my family from so-called second hand smoke.

No, not because of those ass holes that raised tobacco taxes thru the roof.

No, not because it is a filthy habit with ash trays, matches, lighters etc. I sort of liked them.

In my fifth grade class we had large charts that were depictions of the human body without skin. The one on the right showed us a healthy naked man. The one on the left showed a similar naked man who apparently smoked ten packs a day for a lifetime. His guts were painted brown with nicotine and other shit.

Nothing was said about the soothing action on the brain of even mild hints of this drug. All good drugs are bad if you overuse or abuse them, even aspirin, caffeine, sleeping pills, tranquilizers and pot.

My advice for smoking was simple:

- Do not inhale.
- Don't carry cigarettes with you.
- Never smoke while reclining.
- Buy the weakest cigs you can get.
- Don't smoke before eleven A.M, and no more than a pack a day.
- Always tell waiters and barmen you've not been around their   place of business lately because of the stupid smoking bans.

Tobacco has been a comfort for almost 500 years. If it used wisely and with the proper limitations it can add to the enjoyment of life.

I once told my Doc that since my blood pressure was way too low that I smoked to raise it a bit in social events so as not to be a lump on a log. His advice: Eat more salt! And he still charged me for that lame advice.

When Japanese attacked Pearl Harbor we declared war on Japan.

When Saudis attacked New York we declared war on Iraq. YES?

Wife: "The young lady next door is looking for a husband."

Husband: "I'm one."

Condoms are now 99% effective. So, if you have sex twice a week, you'll only get pregnant once a year.

ADVICE TO THE LOVE WORN

Some women talk-show pun-dits say that men are simple, all they are interested in is steak and sex. Sur! When a man [or woman] leaves the high stress action and brain power lightening of the workplace and arrives home, he has to shift down, be simple and thus he is easily pleased. Tough at work, simple at home. It keeps him sane. If he were simple at work and tough at home, she'd be angry. Simple is better.

Even Fake Fur wants to live!

CHAPTER 64 - SOULS

We may have souls. They might be located in the part of the brain that contains the conscience. However, many people have almost no conscience, so maybe they don't have a soul. One thing is scientifically sure – a soul could not survive more than a few minutes outside our head. Everything that is alive needs FUEL.

NAM

The war in Nam was an extension of the Korean War. Both wars were meant to stop the tide of communism and both fulfilled their aim. The Red Tide had gobbled up about a dozen countries in Europe and Asia and we [Harry Truman] meant to put a stop to the spreading cancer. After WWII, four areas were left half communist and half free. These were Germany, Berlin, Korea, and Viet Nam. First the Reds tried to take over West Berlin, and Truman devised the Berlin Air Lift. The Reds backed down. Then they invaded South Korea and Truman sent in our troops. After four years the Reds wanted an armistice. Then they invaded South Viet Nam and again we resisted. They broke the Peace Treaty but they never again tried to take over another nation. They found these wars to be so expensive as to be untenable and the economics of the communist way was revealed as a failure around the world.

But the dictators of China and Cuba still like it. In Cuba, everyone but Castro knows that Communism keeps them poor. The Chinese leaders will discover, just like the Russians, that Communism keeps the economy DOWN.

I believe that the Kremlin Kooks finally got the message via their collective farms. Whatever they grew or raised, they had to deliver it to the collective market and take whatever was given them. But: they were allowed to have a small plot of their own. And guess where they put all their efforts? It was "free enterprise."

CHAPTER 65 - INTRODUCTIONS TO BAR BELLS

On the assumption that most women in bars are there for the same reason men are, or, "if you're not here after what I'm here after, you   will still be here after I'm gone," philosophy, the following are the winning opening lines when one is introducing oneself to a Bar Bell:

"I was invited to this high class party and I'm supposed to bring a classy date, could you make it?"

"Is it hot in here or is it you?"

"Do you think you could care for our kids?"

"How would you like to visit my planet?"

"You are real pretty and I'm real shy."

DROP OUTS

If school drop-outs should accidentally venture into polite society they will find that most of the conversation goes right over their heads. But they won't even realize it. Their attitude: "So what?"

THE LEARNING CURVE FOR BANK ROBBERS

A young unemployed drop-out decided to rob a bank because he found a toy pistol that looked real. He bought a ski-mask with his last ten bucks and walked into a bank and shouted, "Hands up, you mother stickers, this is a fuck-up!"

A NONSEQUITOR

15,000 babies are born every hour and the whole population of the earth could reside in Texas, but -------?

CHAPTER 66 - THE LIFE TIME DIET

This theory proposes that everyone has a capacity to engorge just so many calories in their lifetime. Ergo, if you eat them too fast you will die young. But if you stretch them out [eat less] you can live to be a hundred.

People who make a living writing DIET books, could wriggle this idea out into 350 pages, and all the people who wished they were slimmer would pay $20 for it, not read it and feel better.

Yes, 350 pages to say: Eat less = live longer. $20 saved.

CRADLE ROBBERS

I once asked a middle aged bachelor why he always dated young girls instead of women his own age. He said, "It's simple. Young girls are playing hard to get, while women my age are obsessed with sex. You can never satisfy them. A man needs a rest now and then."

Of course, on the other side of the coin, the ladies who have hit the maximum of "hornyness" should date teen-agers who are "peaking."

CHAPTER 67 - OXYGEN

Oxygen is like sex, it's not important unless you're not getting any.

My first encounter with the possible dangers of oxygen happened back right after the big War when all the airlines were in a rush to buy new airliners. Old time mechanics told many stories about bad accidents that had happened in aviation manufacturing. One tale was about how to install oxygen bottles in the cargo bay of the new DC-6s and Constellations by Douglas and Lockheed. One old guy told me about the mechanic who unscrewed the top off such a big bottle, thinking it was empty. The uncapped bottle became a five foot rocket and shot out of the cargo bay and across the yard. Another guy told me that mechanics always put a dab of grease on the big cap nuts to make it easier to install. But, he warned, if you do that to an oxygen bottle, the compressed oxygen will spontaneously combust and give you either a bomb or a blow torch. Apparently, compressed oxygen will burn or flame up whenever it comes in contact with anything organic. This includes plants and animals but not minerals. So then, if you should drop a live rat into a container of compressed oxygen, it would burn like a torch.

Before the moon trip in 1969, NASA had the bright idea to fill the astronauts' capsule, the rocket cabin, with compressed oxygen then the three men in the space ship wouldn't have to wear oxygen masks. Some one should have asked those old mechanics I mentioned previously. This was a bad idea. If you remember the headlines of the day, the three men caught on fire and burned up quickly. It was a costly and sad lesson

AUTO EFFICIENCY

An old French mechanic once remarked that it took a certain amount of energy to move a given weight up to a certain speed. And that if you wanted better gas mileage in your car, you would have to reduce its weight. An engineering formula says: $F = Ma$. This means that the force required to accelerate something is equal to the mass of the object multiplied by the desired acceleration. So, for a desired acceleration, you can achieve it by using more fuel [more force] or less mass [or weight].

So we find that dinky little foreign cars are not more efficient, they are just made with thinner steel. Does this mean less safety? Believe it!

RED NECKS' GUNS

Few advocate removing guns from private hands, but guns probably should be registered just like our cars. Rednecks keep quoting PART of the Second Amendment which has to do with arming militias. On several occasions in the last thirty years, the Supreme Court has ruled that local governments can regulate firearms any way they like.

FOR PEAT'S SAKE

Peat is the preferred fuel of Ireland, but the United States has peat fields three times the entire land area of Ireland. Our Department of Energy spent five years and $40 million on research to find the best way to convert peat into gas. Then the Reagan administration found us so far in debt that it cut out these studies. The state of Minnesota alone has more energy available from peat than the entire U.S. oil reserves.   U figger.

DEFICITS

To remove government deficits you either have to increase taxes or reduce government. Is that so hard?

CHAPTER 68 - NOT TOO VERBOSE

I grew up as the youngest kid in a family with a brother and two sisters. In order to get in my two cents worth, I would gather my thoughts, condense them and when there was an opening, and spew them out in a quick stream. This worked well at home and at school, but in later corporate life I found that such a short dose of concise information would usually go over the bosses head while he was settling down expecting a long harangue.

The one boss who was not snowed by my staccato bursts of rhetoric was a man with an Ivy League Engineering degree and a Phi Beta Kappa key on his vest. At a luncheon, he remarked to a cohort that my humor was not burlesque but "music hall." I chewed over that for a nonce.

In elementary school during the great depression, I assumed that a yellow ruled tablet provided me in September was to last until June, therefore I learned to write very small, and sometimes with several topics on the same page, perish forbid I would discard a sheet before it was full.

Getting back to this aforementioned boss; once I handed him an idea about aircraft financing written musingly in the middle of a yellow tablet sheet containing other notes and jots. My far-out idea was that with the current inflation [circa 1967] we could blend the projected inflation rate into the return-on-investment calculations to show that this kind of inflation would help pay off the airplane and we might as well take advantage of it.

A week later he returned my yellow sheet with a nice note saying that the corporate finance gurus apparently couldn't understand anything so simple or revolutionary. But thanks!

I felt that I had at least achieved a breakthrough in paper savings. Huh.

TRUTHS

Your own convictions are your own TRUTHS. But of course, you're only right if you agree with MY truths.

Many of us are sitting on a wide white whale fishing for bait! Is this backwards?

HOW TO BE A MILLIONAIRE

If financial advisors and writers knew how to make you rich do you think they would tell YOU? Why should they? If everyone were suddenly wealthy inflation would make us all poor again.

Well paid forecasters cannot predict the financial future, BU, they are often paid to predict things or trends that will help certain business interests.

ADOPT A PET

Or baby.

Some childless couples adopt a child so as to carry on the family name. Does this make sense? After all, if Mother Nature didn't consider you proper parenting candidates in the first place, will adoption make it so?

Millions of years of fine tuning by Mrs. Nature brings us to the condition where many millionaires are barren while marginal retards are prolific. Go figger.

POETS

You can write poetry or you can write prose, but if it doesn't rhyme, it's just a pose.

WANT AD

Wanted to buy, left legs, will pay up to $1000, deliver to 1137 E. Lombard.

SLAVERY

When Lincoln freed the slaves, none of them tried to shoot him.

[Iraq???]

STOCK MARKET

If you buy stock in a company you are a part owner.

If you buy a company's bonds you are lending them money.

In the event of a bankruptcy, who gets paid off first?

The LENDER!

ETERNITY

Eternity means here and now. Your future is today. This is it – for us.

CHAPTER 69 - OLD TIME RELIGION

Many old people yearn for old time religion. But times they change with the years. Like different kinds of computers, the software for old and new religions are usually not interchangeable.

MEAT EATERS UNITE

Some animals' guts are designed to eat veggies and some are made to eat meat, and a few are designed to eat both. Take for instance, bears, pigs, goats and monkeys and apes. These beasties, and ourselves, are designed to eat both sides of the plate. And if we humans do not eat both, we are not whole, i.e. we lack certain things we need to live and thrive.

Many dog foods are mostly grain products because they're cheaper than meat. They tell you "it's good for them." Did anyone ever see a pack of wolves attack a wheat field?

Carnivores [meat eaters] must have more speed, strength and endurance than the herbivores [vegans] or they couldn't catch them to eat them. And, over the years, they developed the extra cunning required.

Aren't the wolves, dogs, cats, apes, monkeys and bears smarter than the cows, horses, buffaloes, deer, elk, moose etc.? If elephants were smart they wouldn't be working for peanuts. And if our bush ancestors had not learned to scavenge meat from abandoned kills, we would probably be just another extinct species. Remember, 90% of all species that ever evolved became extinct before the advent of man.

CHAPTER 70 - TITLEISTS

What's with medical doctors and their mania to be called by their graduation degree? Other graduates with even more prestigious titles don't usually insist on being called by their occupation notations. I can't imagine calling a man with a Ph.D. in rocket or aerospace sciences being called Doctor. They would laugh [cette a rire]. CEOs, Presidents, Deans, Coaches, and Managers all can be more important than medics.

I've probably known more old doctors than most doctors and I like to call them by their first names because I know that they will call me by my first name as soon as they see me. When they say, "How are you today, Edward?" I answer, "Not too bad, George." Now we are on an even footing and we can go on from there. Sometimes I tell them that most doctors wouldn't last a week in an engineering office because there, you are not allowed to GUESS.

CHAPTER 71 - THE ENERGY OF NATURE

We invent gods to manifest the energy of nature. And Mother Nature doesn't give a damn what we do.

We should all trust in our faith[s] one supposes, but EXPERIENCE is bankable.

Your life is like a play, where you WILL what will happen next, but sometimes the PLOT goes awry and we don't like it. Some people can will it differently.

Some times our lives are journeys that never end. Remembering the journey is the best part because the bad parts get edited out, somehow.

VALHALLA

A martyred Arab sent a message from Valhalla to the comrades he had left behind on earth: It said, "It's not 72 virgins that you get, it's a 72 year old virgin."

All stars are raging nuclear furnaces, and some are as wide as from here to our sun.

Some elections end up choosing the evil of two lesser.

White Folks Alert: Four kids are enough, remember, every fifth baby born in the world is Chinese.

CHAPTER 72 - WHEN THE WORLD WAS FLAT

Once in a while, maybe every thousand years or so, we should be entitled to some new Gawds. The ones we have now were invented by unsophisticated MEN who thought the world was flat, and who thought the sun revolved around the earth. The world and its sciences have evolved so far ahead of those guys that we should no longer be stuck with their rules.

The old Ten Commandments were over 500 words long, as I remember, and many of them seemed to have been trying to establish the importance of the God in question. I don't remember seeing the word "tolerance" anywhere. So when anyone gets around to writing a new book on human conduct and morality, its first word should be TOLERANCE.

Many writers have noted that Morality is hard to define to everyone's satisfaction. Of the billions of people on this earth, maybe they could come up with a billion definitions of morality. Maybe you will know it when you see it.

Many years ago, I wrote a new bible for my new religion, not a religion, just rules to live by, if you agree with the rules. My Book only had one page. That is all that was needed.

[I wonder where I put that page]

BALBOA BLVD, BALBOA PARK, BALBOA ISLAND ETC.

I recently noted that a man named Nunez had been named head of the county supervisors or some such. I called his office to get his exact address and then wrote him a nice letter of congratulations and also mentioned that I wondered if he knew about his famous ancestor who was a Spanish explorer who "discovered" the Pacific Ocean a long time ago.

In those days a Spanish Grandee was called by both his father's and his mother's family name. Ergo, his official name would be Nunez y Balboa. The latter being his mother's family name. I suggested in my letter that he be a committee of one to rename all those places currently called Balboa to the proper cognomen: NUNEZ. He must have thought I was kidding, as he never answered.

We used to answer every letter out of courtesy, which is now dead along with etiquette. May they Rest In Peace. RIP

CHAPTER 73 - MIRACLES

An old fart said it best when he was blasting the Catholic Church back in 1855. William Money said: "Miracles are for the ignorant and barbarous who cannot be enlightened by arguments." There probably has never been a miracle by scientific standards. Of course ten inches of rain in the Sahara desert may seem to some like a miracle but it's more likely just some errant clouds that make such a mistake every thousand years.

Around 150 years ago a peon near Mexico City said that the Virgin Mary [or Marie] came and spoke to him in a flash of light. So they built a church on the spot. At the time they probably had lots of time and money and needed a new miracle. If such a peasant said the same thing today, what would the priests do?

EXERCISE

For Father's Day, a guy got some in-line skates and a treadmill. So he used them both at once and made everybody happy.

YOUR HEAD

If you live in your head you've got it all; what more do you need? But some people's heads gets too big to live in. However, anyone can get rid of massive egotism by being self-defecating.

BIRTH CONTROL

Why do the people who can least afford it have the most kids?

Because they're DUMB! Or, smart enough to get more welfare.

CHAPTER 74 - OLD COLONELS ARE NICE TO KNOW

It is an old military custom. If you write a document that asks for something, you must submit it to the guy above you in rank. If he agrees, he "endorses" it by adding his signature and forwarding it on to the next highest decision-maker until finally it is approved or rejected. It works. Each guy passes the "buck" until someone like an old Colonel okays it. Then "The Buck Stops Here." Therefore, everyone in military service would be wise to get on the good side of an Old Colonel. Any request that you make in writing, if endorsed by an old Colonel will be approved.

I was smaller than average when I started High School, but I joined the R.O.T.C. because my older brother had done so and besides you got to wear the uniform three days a week and good clothes were hard to come by in the Big Depression. Then I amazed myself by getting on the Rifle Team and being the best marksman in my school.

Thus, I caught the eye of the Old Colonel that ran the joint. I went from private to corporal to sergeant to captain to major. The other guys on the team all wore sharpshooter medals except me. They cost fifteen cents and for that kind of money I could go to three movies, buy three hot dogs, or ride the ferry across the Mississippi three times. Those medals came from the National Riflemakers Association. They're up to no good.

As a freshman in college Senior ROTC I was made a corporal the first month and also made the Rifle Team. Then in the second year I went all the way to Sergeant Major, the highest rank available for that year. That caught the Old Colonel's eye. As a senior, I was presented with a gold medal by the state governor signifying the best Captain in 22 companies. So later, when I petitioned for a deferment of active duty to finish my college courses, the Old Colonel endorsed my request and it was approved.

Nobody can argue with a "Bird Colonel" except a General.

Before the year was up I applied, through channels, to be assigned to flight training in the Army Air Corps. Granted. The Old Colonel again. So I went to Texas to fly. I already had a Pilot's License so the flying part wasn't difficult, but in advanced flight training I came down with the Flu and couldn't finish with my class. So I had to go see an Old Colonel to decide what to do with me.

He said, "I see you are an Aeronautical Engineer. They need guys like you at Wright Field in Dayton, Ohio; maybe I'll send you there."

His aide said, "You're not allowed to do that."

The Old Colonel said, "What can they do to me?"

So I ended up in the place that was busy buying about 10,000 airplanes. I was there only a week when an Old Colonel needed to replace some Captain who had gone bananas so he picked me to be a department head. I found I was in charge of the typing pool of about 40 females. They were all staring at me, very unsettling. So I picked out the ugliest one in the bunch, and gave her a raise. Everyone smiled and went back to work.

After a while I sent a memo to my boss, a young Colonel, and asked to be taken out of the Hen House and be put to work as an Engineer. He grinned and said yes. Now, still a Lieutenant, I was sent out to the factories that were making bombers and fighters and (A) see if they were following the rules in building planes, and (B) try to help them with any problems.

I must have been doing O.K. because the Old Colonel never complained, even when I blew a few thousand. On one visit I was told to evaluate the inspection operations run by an Old Colonel at a bomber factory. I advised my office to fire him and he was transferred the next day. The next factory I visited, the Old Colonel in charge had his rest pilots take me up in a B-29. What a thrill! Next it was a B-24, and then a ride in a two-seater P-47. Wow!

Then in Los Angeles, when the contractor threw a banquet for me at Earl Carrol's Dinner Theatre, I suspected maybe they were being too nice to me. Meanwhile, when I returned to my office, a Light Colonel whom I had never met, dropped by and asked if I would be interested in attending the fabulous Command and General Staff School at Ft. Leavenworth, Kansas, for 13 weeks. I said I believed that school was only for Captains and above. He said to try it anyhow. I made the application, my Old Colonel endorsed it and I was in.

The Command and General Staff School was what it must have been like in the prewar army. We were housed in two story brick mansions that Old Colonels and Generals lived in during peacetime. Private rooms and a bat man to shine your shoes and make your bed. A bus to take you to class, then to lunch, then back to class etc. And week ends off to go to Kansas City.

Then all of a sudden the war was over. We finished our class work and returned to our previous condition of servitude. Almost all of the officers in my old department had left the service and I received a notice to travel to Salt Lake City preparatory to being sent to Tokyo to be part of General Macarthur's occupation staff. After a month in a fancy Mormon hotel, an old Colonel called me in and said that since I had a wife and two little boys, I would have to volunteer to go, or be separated from the army.

Well, I declined to volunteer, but asked if I could stay in my old office in Dayton for sixty days to send out resumes because with the war over, it might be tough to get a job in aviation. He okayed it and I did get a job as Stress Engineer at Northrup. And everybody lived happily.

So, I joined the Love Old Colonels Organization (LOCO).

CHAPTER 75 - FAIR TRADE

Asians do not believe in fair trade. They think it is proper to corner the market in their particular sphere. In their regimes it is logical to sell below costs until the competition is bankrupted. One can only sell at a loss if your fellows in the field will support your efforts, but lacking this you must have your government's support.

That is why cars exported to us from Asia COST LESS HERE THAN THEY DO IN ASIA. FAIR trade requires a level playing field – but – that is a western idea and not normal to the Far East.

Engineers get no respect because they are of an experimental design.

Depression is all in your head.

She wore black garters in memory of the boys who had gone beyond.

BAD LUCK

Any Geologist can tell you about the history of the earth.

Any Astronomer can tell you about the history of the universe.

Any Anthropologist can tell you about the history of man.

They will all tell you that superstition is bad luck.

SOCCER

Baseball and football have so many rules that young children should not be subjected to these sports until they can understand all the vagaries.

Basketball and soccer are simple and designed for all ages.

Maybe that's why our elementary schools have the lower grades play soccer or basketball until such time as they are ready for something that requires more brain power.

CHAPTER 76 – JOKES

If the British had won the Revolutionary War, we would all be British, with socialized medicine, no pistols, and closed borders.

Speaking of the British, they sometimes have a sense of humor. Some British tourists were late in arriving at the tourist part of Auschwitz. The guard was closing the gate so one of the tourists got out of the car to argue their way in. He was getting no where with the stern German guard so one of the other men in the car stuck his head out of the car window and shouted, "Tell him we're Jewish."

Latinos in the U.S. should be patient. Soon they will be the majority, and then they will be in charge of their own WELFARE just as in Latin America.

Political discussions usually try to ignore the FACTS.

If Lawmakers' sons were drafted first in wartime, and if the materiel for the military were confiscated from the factories – who would want to go to war? Unless, of course, if we were invaded.

Most people are willing to sacrifice and give up some of their liberties during wartime. But not WHEN WE START THE WAR!

Some say Kerry threw away his war medals. We wonder if Little Bush will do the same.

People who don't read are just as smart as people who can't read.

Elevators play uplifting music

CHAPTER 77 - YOUR BRAIN

I believe that when you die, Heaven Forbid, your brain follows a prepared course for a blink in time where we can see flashes of all the scenes we were expecting. Your brain can do this in a fraction of a second.

Mine might take a whole second.

Then, with no blood cells to feed it, it will start to decay [rot]. This is usually called "Brain Damage." The End

GAYETY IN MARRIAGE

Some people want to pass a law that says a marriage can only be between a man and a woman, presumably to fit their own narrow moral standards. I guess that it would be all right for a woman to marry a woman if she were in a man's body. Or vice versa.

Remember, before criticizing someone else you should walk a mile in their shoes. Then, when you do criticize them, you will be a mile away from them, and, you will have their shoes.

Feminists are sooo cute!

No husband has ever been shot while doing the dishes.

A few hundred years ago everybody was stupid and the earth WAS flat.

ANY set of words is a bad set of words if they keep us from the harmless pursuit of happiness.

Choose one:

God can do anything but doesn't care,

God cares but can't do everything.

CHAPTER 78 - WEIRD BANK CHARGES

On two of my Bank of America monthly statements, there was a weird charge of about $60 that I didn't understand. So I called and was told by a nice lady that it concerned a magazine distributor's charge. As I sputtered, she gave me the company's phone number; she must have had it right at her fingertips. So I called them. They said it was for my National Enquirer subscription. I said, "I didn't ask for it, had never read it, I didn't want it and how could you do such a criminal thing?" They said, "We will refund your money today."

SO, they already had my money from the bank! Surely the bank wouldn't let them do this unless they got a cut of the action. And I only discovered it because it was on a card I had never used! Also, the bank charged me $5 for their inconvenience! What about mine?

I'm no Einstein, but I feel like a Redneck arguing about chickens in a prenuptial agreement.

Maybe if you other B of A customers will send a copy of this to them with your next payment? LET'S REBEL!

CHAPTER 79 - THE LATE DEAR ABBY

A while back, Dear Abby published a letter of mine on a Saturday, a day when it is not published in the *L.A. Times*. Some one sent me a copy from the Moline Dispatch. Since no one locally has read it, and since it has to do with ageing, it might be of interest.

Dear Abby: Ever since I've reached my eighties (88) my mail is full of health products designed to help me live longer. I once had many friends, all of whom were health vigilantes. They shook their heads knowingly as I avoided all strenuous labor and exercise. They made liquids out of good vegetables and spent fortunes on the latest food supplements. They argued that "organic" was better and "natural" was best. I would tell them that snake venom, poison ivy and manure were all natural but they wouldn't listen. Now they're all dead and I have no one left to argue with.

Eddy Hill

Sherman Oaks, Calif.

Dear Eddy: The secret to longevity may be a well developed sense of humor. Tis said, "He who laughs, lasts."

Abby

CHAPTER 80 - THE WEAKER SEX

In human evolution, some sects split off and developed differently than the others. Sometimes they were stronger; sometimes they became extinct in a few hundred years. One group developed women who were bigger and stronger than the men. Excess young men and boys were shunted off to cope for themselves. The women did the hunting because they were better at it. The women only became pregnant when it was their idea and they wanted to have a child. The number of births diminished until the tribe could not sustain its numbers. The elder women debated their problem and asked the ones of child bearing age to contribute, but these young girls had excuses and more pleasant things to do. Without the male libido to woo the women and the male sex drive to power the necessary seductions, the tribe became extinct. Listen up, lassies.

REPAIR THE BASICS

The Good Old USA is falling apart. It is always intriguing to build something new, but it's boring to keep it up or repair it.

We have eroding roads.

Our mass transit is messy.

We have poor power grids.

Our water systems are waning.

We have sinking sewers.

Our old schools are a shame.

Our parks have grown poor.

And the rush hour traffic starts before noon.

CHAPTER 81 - OUR CONGESTED FREEWAYS CAN BE DOUBLE DECKED

I once asked a Caltrans Freeway Design Engineer why they were not espousing double-decks to solve the freeway congestion problem. He replied, "We can double-deck, just get us the budget." Apparently, it would cost much less to erect a second roadway above the existing freeways than it would to buy up land and buildings and relocate residents and businesses.

I believe it would not be much of a challenge for Mechanical and Civil Engineers to design an "eye pleasing" sturdy upper road bed which would NOT tie up more than one lane of traffic during the construction hours. The towers and hinged roadway could be manufactured off-site to be delivered and assembled a section at a time.

Such a design would double the number of vehicle lanes and would incorporate on-off ramps as needed. The work could proceed at a rational pace, beginning with the worst bottle-neck areas.

CHAPTER 82 - JIBES

1st person; "It's a pleasure to meet you."

2nd person: "Oh yeah? Just wait 'til you get to know me!"

First Texan [in a bar]: "My ranch is so big that if I start out on one end at dawn, in my car, I won't get to the other end until sunset."

Second Texan: "I used to have a car like that."

In Pennsylvania, two young squirts were driving down a country road when they came upon an Amish girl, all in black. One oaf leaned out the car window and addressed the young lady: "Miss, is it true that you Amish girls don't wear any underwear beneath those long black dresses?"

She replied: "Screw Thee."

Everyone should learn Spanish because some day you will want to hire a gardener, or a Governor...

I hired two Latinos once who were supposed to be adept at applying outside stucco. My son, Roger, had obtained their services for me. When they were finished, I was not pleased so I tried to explain in Spanish that the new stucco did not look the same as the rest of the house.

I said, "*Esta no es le mismo.*"

They shook their heads and looked dumb. Just then my son arrived. He took one look and said, "That's a piece of shit; do it over!"

They said, "YESSIR" and jumped back to work.

The cost of living keeps going up, but it's still popular.

A mirage is not an optical illusion, it just looks like one.

If swimming is so good for your figure, how do you explain whales?

CHAPTER 83 - EVOLUTION

Evolution progresses not only by beneficial mutations but also by accommodation to animal practices. For instance, if we domesticate dogs and cats for thousands of years, eventually they are born with an easy adaptability to human association.

After thousands of years of our refining the art of speech, our babies are born with the ability to readily learn to speak.

No one will be born with a "basketball sized brain" because of the limitation to the female bone structure. However, when humans learned to talk, our brain power increased dramatically, thereby causing our heads to expand. That is why the only animal that screams during birthing is the human female.

A Jehovahs Witness asked me, "If you believe in evolution, why don't you go down to the Zoo and watch a monkey turn into a man?"

I answered, "Who's got fifty million years to spend at the Zoo?"

Evolution is not a theory, it is the facts of our history. Our evolutionary history is filled with life, death, suspense, mystery, surprises, and sex in a thousand different ways. And almost unbelievable tragedies. It precedes nations and religions by a couple billion years.

Evolution explains who we are, how we got here, and to where we're probably going.

We have found the remains of giant beasts that have lasted a million years longer than we have. Why were they so successful and why did they die out? History is never finished.

Can anyone fanaticize about the fireside stories our ancestors told their children 10,000 years ago? They probably assumed that "This is as good as it will get." Their stories enriched their kids' lives long before the Genesis stories were ever told. The many concepts of God evolved along with all the other cultural knowledge and myths.

Even in primitive times their stories of 'yesterday' improved the minds of 'today.'

An essay by Paul Gordon on evolution was refreshingly disingenuous. I imagine that when his father was a boy and was asked to add two apples and two apples, he asked, "What apples?"

Evolution progresses not only by beneficial mutations but also by accommodation to animal practices. For instance, if we domesticate dogs and cats for thousands of years, eventually they are born with an easy adaptability to human association.

CHAPTER 84 - HOW WAS THE FOOD?

Where ever you travel around the world, when you return, friends and neighbors are interested for about three minutes as you explain the excitement of snake charmers in Morocco or sexy dancers in Rio or the beer halls of Germany or the circus of Moscow or the sun bathers of Bali etc, etc, etc. They are quick to ask: "How was the food?"

I usually answer, "We didn't go there to eat."

But since food seems to be the dominant interest in some people's lives, I could list a few food finds that surprised...

STEAK: Los Angeles, Pacific Dining Car, West Sixth Street (If it's still there)

LEMON CHICKEN: Hong Kong, Jade Garden, near the Hilton

VEAL CUTLET: Orleans, France. Le Cremelliere, by the river. The meat was covered with a slab of parsley butter. White table cloths.

INDONESIAN SHRIMP: San Miguel d'Allende, Mexico. Le Jardin restaurant on the main square. Shrimp is rolled in shredded coconut, deep fried, and hung over the side of half a pineapple full of cognac sauce.

ENCHILADA RANCHERO: Sherman Oaks [Los Angeles] Casa Vega, Ventura and Fulton. Ala carte with sour cream.

LOBSTER: Vancouver, Canada, Bayside Inn by the bay.

PORK TENDERLOIN sandwich: Davenport, or Donahue, Iowa. This breaded delight is epicurean.

HAM HOCKS AND SAUERKRAUT: Any place in Dusseldorf, Germany

CHAPTER 85 - THE GENTLEMEN'S CODE

If you assume a guy is a gentleman and you loan him something and he does not return it, it is worth the loss to find out that he is not a gentleman. It says here.

This life's little lesson landed in my lap once. I met a man whose kids played with my kids. I visited his house one time and learned that he was unemployed having been fired as a vice president of some big ad company, like Burto, Barton, Durston & Osborn whatever. He was a quiet gracious man.

About ten years later he appeared at my door and asked to borrow three hundred dollars, I gave it to him and he departed. Note: In dealings like this you do NOT say, "Why do you need it? When do I get it back?" You either loan it to him or you don't.

Later, I casually mentioned to some strangers what had happened and they said I was a fool and that I'd never see that money again. About six weeks later the gentleman again appeared at my door and repaid the loan. We had little in common to talk about, just "Thank You" and that was it. I've since heard that he, his wife and kids have all passed away.

Another part of The Gentleman's Code applies to romantic affairs. One may regale others with tales of two-bit tarts and trifling trysts with tolerable tramps, but a gentleman never lets on he loved a Lady. Even under oath.

Visionary, "I have ESP."

Double Visionary, "I have ESPN."

In politics, the opposite of Left is not Right, and the opposite of Right is not Left. The opposite of both is the Center.

The hardest job in life is to weigh an issue without a preconceived idea.

It has been suggested that Michael Jackson could solve all his problems by becoming a priest.

Some men's problems are caused by the fact that the source of their testosterone is so far from the brain and so close to the butt.

Many Frenchmen like to have a few Escargot with their meals, but they will never be as popular here because they will never be 'fast' food.

A TV cameraman was being interviewed and he was asked about the Reality show he worked on. He was asked how he fared on this deserted land where everyone had to find their own food and water or die. He answered that his union contract assured that the crew would have a full buffet table available at all times.

CHAPTER 86 - AFFAIRS OF THE BRAIN

Today, a person's sexual definition is determined by their plumbing. This custom is not always fair because a person's sexual orientation will decide how they should conduct themselves, because of our beliefs.

BELIEFS as such, are not natural laws no matter how much 'faith' is Involved.

BELIEFS can make people fly airplanes into tall buildings, and, can skew some government policies so that they no longer represent the public's best interests.

Dictators' faiths have always subverted civil rights.

UNREFINED HUMOR

There is no polite way to complain of the passing of gas. Try this : "Thank you for that flat you lent us."

You can't just go and buy a door knocker, you have to buy two. Knockers always come in pairs.

The early bird gets the worm, but the second mouse gets the cheese.

Join the Army, meet new people, kill them.

If you believe in psycho kinesis, raise my hand.

Royalty are people who are paid to be better than the people who pay them.

Why does Noah's Ark always have pointed ends?

If there is intelligent life on Earth it is spread very thin.

"Why do I drink? It makes you interesting."

The reason there are few fights at protest marches - the sensible side is at work.

Be a Robin Hood. It is easier to take from the rich than work.

Money can't buy brains or class.

One school principle said that if the only adjective you know is:

"COOL," you're a very dull conversationalist.

George W., Ronald and Arnold all found out that you could reduce taxes by borrowing the money to run the government. So, if we borrowed it ALL, there would be NO taxes.

"My ancestors were all German, but they were only following orders."

If the people in our southern states want their own flag, why don't they start their own country?

CHAPTER 87 - THE PREEMPTIVE U.S. [us]

If we are going to be a preemptive, aggressive nation, why should we spend trillions for a missile defense system?

It would be a lot cheaper to just find out who is building missiles and bomb the shit out of them.

Besides, once capable enemies find out we finally have a missile defense that works [50 years from now], they will put their missiles on cargo ships and park them off shore and our expensive system in Alaska etc, would be as obsolete as an Edsel.

OUTSOURCEING

Just think how much profit that corporate America could make if we privatized our military establishment. It has already started.

NUCLEAR WASTE DISPOSAL

No one wants trains or trucks to go through their town on the way to Yucca Mountain. Okay, maybe this stuff should all be transported by cargo planes. It would cost less than building new tracks or roads to bypass every town along the way. Then I suppose some stupid ape would holler, "Don't fly over my house!"

POTUS

When a new President of the United States [Potus] finds out just how powerful he is, some of them are tempted to use it. These lesser men give in to the siren song and send our armed forces against some one, just for the fun of it. A big ego trip. The biggest. And sometimes it is used in the hope that it will get them reelected.

CHAPTER 88 - RELIGIOSITY

Life makes us learn that religion is not the answer, it's the PROBLEM. In matters of the occult, we are a retrograde country. Have we not found that all beliefs have consequences? No belief is worthwhile if it cannot stand up to scientific inspection.

SEX

No God would be so provincial as to peek into all the world's bedrooms, constantly?

WHEEL BARROWS

When the old books were written, Bible, Torah, Koran etc, wheel barrows were considered High-Tech

NEW LIFE

Biologists will tell us that there probably has been no new life created for a billion years or so. In animals such as we, a female is born with all the eggs she will ever have and each egg contains part of her life and when it presents itself for fertilization, if she neglects to do so, she is aborting that microscopic spark of life.

Conception is normally the result of a sexual coupling, but many lab students have found that males are not totally necessary. Parthenogenesis is a nasty word and hard to spell, so forget it, it means that we men aren't needed.

CHAPTER 89 - QUIPS AND QUIDS

Texas Cop: "You got any I. D.?"

Texan: "About what?"

It's been said that some heirs to the throne are born, covered with ermine, while others are covered with just hair of the dog. [All hat and no cows]

There are many ways to die, like old age, murder , sewer side, falling rocks, snake bite etc, etc, but if you die in a hospital they will say that it was a "theropeutic [?] misadventure"

Harpo is Oprah spelled backwards, but they have nothing in common.

CHAPTER 90 - COUNTRY MUSIC

If you are sad or depressed try playing some country music BACKWARDS.

You will get out of jail, your dog will get better and your woman will come home.

UNFAIR

The game of life is unfair, but you can't win unless you play the game.

Adam: "Shall we celebrate Fat Tuesday?"

Eve: "No, let's go to the Mardi Gras."

Parisian: "How do you like the Pate' de Fois Gras?"

New Yorker: "It ain't chopped liver."

THE STATE OF THE UNION

I saw my first Reader's Digest in a Dentist's office in the 1930s. I was quite impressed by one item in it. It was an interview with a hundred year old man. He was asked, "What do you think of the world today?"

He replied, "For as long as I can remember, this country has been going to the dogs."

It is a thought to remember.

ABORTIONS

Those who fight both abortions and contraceptives are like those who are against both disease and medicine.

SEDUCTIVE BODIES

Women can gain a little, lose a little, but never be satisfied with her boobs, belly, bottom or thighs. What matters is what a man imagines he can do with the parts you do have.

PUZZLES

If a light sleeper can sleep better with a light on, couldn't a hard sleeper sleep better with a window open?

If a quiz is quizzical, then a test is   -   ?

What country is the most aggressive, has the most debt, is the most undereducated, the most over weight, has the most gun deaths and has the highest priced drugs?   My country tis of thee…

A SONG WITHOUT A TUNE

If you're not feeling up to par,

Never let it show.

Those who ask you how you are,

Don't really want to know.

DOING THE POOCH

A sharply dressed matron was walking her dog, a Pit Bull, in the park when she stopped to answer the cell phone in her purse. It was playing a classic concerto. Her conversation must have been engaging as it was quite protracted. Her dog became so bored with the wait and feeling of ennui that he lay down and started licking his balls.

When the lady concluded her casual phone call she put her cell back in her purse. About that time, a bum on a nearby bench pointed to the dog's dainty doings and remarked, "Boy, that looks like fun; I wish I could do that."

The lady glanced at the bum and at the dog and replied, "It's all right with me, but I think you should pet him first."

CHAPTER 91 - FUNERALS

At a funeral, the pastor kept going on and on about the deceased, how he such a good family man, hard worker, good provider etc. The widow prodded one of her sons and said, "Run up there and see if that's your daddy in that box."

A couple was all dressed up for a funeral. The wife had on a nice dress, she had just had her hair done and she was wearing makeup for the first time in years.

Her husband said, "You look so hot we have to have sex before we go."

She said ,"Not now."

He said, "We're not going unless we do."

She said, "Oh all right, what do you want me to take off, gloves, girdle or lipstick?"

People used to make jokes about men laying in their coffins. It was probably the only time they got dressed up. In 1925 some one wrote a song about it :

When you're all dressed up and no place to go,

Life seems weary, dreary and slow,

My heart has ached and bled,

For the tears I've shed, But there's no place to go,

Unless I go back to bed.

I've had a sad sad life and whenever I go,

To that peaceful spot where the violets grow,

There'll be a nice white stone,

Where it's written below,

He was all dressed up but no place to go.

CHAPTER 92 - OUR ELECTORAL COLLEGE

It used to take our leaders weeks to travel to a congressional session. I think it was Andrew Jackson who complained that it took him two weeks to travel from Tennessee to Washington by horse and buggy because there were no roads.

In national elections there was no way the 'popular votes' could be sent to D.C. and counted. Unless one was willing to wait several months. Therefore the idea was conceived to have an 'Electoral College" where each colony

would be represented by electors who would do the voting for us, proportionate to the amount of the state's eligible voters (all men, all white).

Some day we will have an amendment to vote by computer and let the 'popular vote' win. Of course the weaker states will try to interfere with the passage of such an amendment for as long as their money for lobbyists holds out.

In a democracy your vote counts, but under feudalism your Counts voted...

CHAPTER 93 - CAMPAIGN FINANCING

All politicians who feed at the tax money trough want to keep the current corrupt status quo. So any changes could never get through by normal legislative means. However, if all reelection contributions were funneled in to the respective party headquarters, it could then be divided equally between all of that party's contenders. Then it would no longer be a bribe, maybe.

This kind of legislation could be adopted by the States through their referendum systems. It would take a lot of work.

The legality of such laws would probably be challenged in court and then even judges would be inclined to call it 'unconstitutional' so as to preserve the present corrupt status quo.

IN A NEW YORK MINUTE

What is it? It's the same length of time as a west-of-the-Mississippi minute of ten years ago. While the sun appears to move from East to West, new ideas, styles and popular humor always seem to move from West to East. New York TV shows such as Saturday Nite Live seem to use humor that was aborning ten years ago, written by the gag writers of L.A., or Lala Land.

Maybe the reason for this is because NY is the biggest collection of small towns outside of India. And a survey discovered that most Yorkers seldom leave an area of about eight blocks around their tenements. Why should they leave when they believe they are at the Center of the Earth (the same as most jungle tribesmen believe)?

Observing youths from that area, when they enroll in mid-western schools, is quite amusing. The locals are so laid back that the easterners, at first, think they're all wimps. Later as they get conditioned to the slower pace, they begin to fit in. Then they become embarrassed at the loud newcomers from the east.

CHAPTER 94 - WRITE TO YOUR CONGRESSMAN

If some one wrote a letter to their lawmaker about a month before the twin towers were going to be demolished and warned that highjackers in four airplaneS would fly them into the towers, what would you suppose would happen? Based on my experience, I would say nothing would happen. Some intern would send you a form letter saying, "thank you for your support and/or suggestions."

In elementary school, our teachers, who knew everything, told us that we can write to the government any time we see something that should be addressed. They also told us about Anarchists. These are the guys who do not write to their congressmen, but try to change the government by bombs, bullets and rebellion. They want to erase all governments.

Our teachers said, "Work through the system, it is the democratic way."

Our politicians say, "We're listening."

After the debacle of 9/11 I found out that no one was listening and nobody cared how many letters you wrote. On November 20th, two months after 9/11 in 2001, it dawned on me that shutting down our airports was like locking the barn after the horse was gone. The terrorists weren't so stupid as to try the same thing twice. And I guessed that the next easy target would be through our ports. So I composed a letter describing how those who wish us harm could knock down the capital dome.

They would put a nice rocket launcher, about as big as a sedan, inside a cargo container that is loaded on a freighter and unloaded along with thousands of others every day at our ports. There it could be transferred into a Mayflower moving van and transported during the night to one of the streets in Washington D.C. that face the capitol building. No one would notice a moving van in the streets of Washington because so many people are coming in and out of government. Then a dozen rockets could bring down our national symbol and the culprits could escape before anyone could organize a defense.

I sent such a letter to the Vice Pres., the Secretary of Defense, the Secretary of State, the Head of the FBI, the head of the CIA, and the Chairman of the Senate Intelligence Committee. I even addressed these letters to the correct numbers on their office doors.

I soon got a reply from the Vice President's office saying that they were forwarding my letter to Tom Ridge in Homeland Security. Then I waited and waited. Three years later and no response. Every year or so I hear some Senator etc. saying something like, "We really ought to do something about the security of our ports."

So don't tell me to write to my congressman, maybe they have lawyers who tell them it is safer to ignore all mail, unless there is a check inside.

Amusingly, when I called an FBI office to get a correct Washington address, the young lady who answered the phone kept giggling and saying: "Stop it, stop it." I wondered why she was telling me that!

CHAPTER 95 - NOBODY LIVES FOREVER

Whether you're into numismatics or gerontology, or if you are an actuary number cruncher, chances are you will be dead in the next ten decades.

HE knew HER before she was a virgin.

THE WRONG SEX

What if God or nature put a person in a body with the wrong plumbing?

The brain of one sex in the body of another? Then that person would be sexually attracted to a brain of the opposite sex, right? So what's the problem?

Marriage is not a RIGHT but it is a RITE invented by people. This rite can be amended by people whenever the current customs change.

THE BIG BANG

Was the universe any different a thousand years before the Big Bang than it was a million, or a billion years before? I realize there were no years back then. And no light-years. And no light. So who cares?

DOG DAYS

A three legged dog walked into an old west saloon and announced: "I'm looking for the man that shot my Paw."

BUDD HISS

The Buddhist in the dentist's chair refused Novocain. He wanted to transcend dental medication.

CHAPTER 96 - WHY THE ATOM WAS NEVER SPLIT

Ancient theologians sometimes posited, "If you have faith as small as a mustard seed etc…" There were many smaller seeds available for their comparison but the little tan, tart mustard seed always made their point..

In the last millennium, there might have been two famous Greeks who could have been thinkers, tailors, bus boys, whatever, called Euripedes and Eumendedese. They made a bet as to who could find the smallest thing in the world. But the challenge was never satisfied. Every time one produced a miniscule speck, or iota of a mote, the other would cut it in two.

The contest continued down through the centuries until the microscope was invented. One was bought by two Greek cousins. One was a girl named Cherry whose school mates renamed her Nonsequitur, Nonny for short. The other was a saucy boy aptly named A-1. They were born to siblings just outside of Wedlock, Pennsylvania. They reveled in the rivalry as they revealed smaller and smaller bits until they realized that they needed a better microscope than the one they had been using in the high school science lab.

They went to their Sears catalogue and ordered the best, the Craftsman model. But soon even that machine's faculties faded when pushed to its outer limits. A-1 said: "Nonny, we must go to a real Sears store and ask one of their experts about this. Surely one of their top-of-the-line-sales-representatives will have a vast knowledge of the ocular eye-light-sensitive-rod enhancement."

As usual, Nonny replied: "Yes."

Sadly, in this new world of commerce, Sears has cashiers but no clerks, so Nonny was forced to observe: "Maybe if we enroll in college and study enough physics courses we will be able to look inside the very atoms of a mustard seed. Then we could see why some sprout and some do not."

A-1 snorted: "Who cares> Mustard seeds are cheap."

Nonny bristled: "You missed the point. I don't think you can cut the mustard!"

And so, ergo, that's why the atom was never split.

CHAPTER 97 - WARS MAKE MEN FAMOUS

If there never was a war, how would young men find an outlet for their natural aggressive natures?

If all young men refused to join or be conscripted into an army some of the most famous men of history might never have been famous.

Alex the Great, the great kings of Medea = Persia = Iran. named Darius, Cyrus and Xerxes, the many Caesars, Napoleon Bonaparte, the several Kaisers [German for Caesar], some Tsars [Russian for Caesar], Hitler, Tojo, Musso, Chaing, Ho and countless others would have been frustrated to sewer side had they had no army to play with.

If we had not started the Revolutionary War we would still be British. So what? With equal representation in Parliament, we of the Americam colonies could vote to move the British capital to New York or some other likely place with a smelly river.

If there had not been a Civil War, slavery would have been sanitized to the nth degree making slaves join a union. When present day blacks whose ancestors refused to be repatriated to Africa after the Civil War start asking for reparations for their ancestor's labor, I say this. What about reparations for me? My great grandparents were slaves in Germany, working without pay or freedom of movement. A lifetime of faithful service sometimes bought them a ticket to America. That's about ten cents a year.

213

If there had been no Spanish American War, William Randolph Hearst could not have built his magic castle, and Puerto Rico people would not be on welfare. And Teddy Roosevelt would still be Governor of New York.

If there had been no World War I, the winners could not have rearranged the old jig saw puzzles into new ones. There was no improvement.

No WW II? The French would have learned to speak German. They might as well; they were also invaded by the 'Huns' in 1870 and 1914. If Germans want to go to Paris that badly, let them. No need for war.

Parisian Husband: "Why do you wear a bra, you have nothing to put in it?"

Wife: "You wear pants, don't you?"

CHAPTER 98 - IF A TREE FALLS

If a tree falls in the forest and no one is there to hear it does it make a sound? Falling trees never make sounds. If there was a running tape recorder when the tipsy tree fell, it would record the variations in air pressure and when the tape was played back, the tape players speaker would make the same air pressure changes and our brains would perceive a signal that we call a sound.

IF the tree fell just right, the air wiggles could make a sound like a hundred piece orchestra playing chopsticks!

Moral: Sounds are only air vibrations.

LIFE IN SPACE

Astronomers have found by spectroscopic analysis that distant space stuff contains all the elements needed for plant and animal life.

CHAPTER 99 – MORE FAMOUS SONGS THAT DIDN'T MAKE IT

If I took you to a dog fight, you'd probably win.

If my nose was full of nickels, I'd blow it all on you.

I used to kiss your lips but it's all over now.

Let me crawl you sweetheart.

Here's a quarter, go call somebody who cares.

If your phone don't ring, you know it's me.

Here's a dollar for a condom so you won't reproduce yourself.

I miss you almost as much as if you were with me.

I can't climb into an upper berth so to you sweetheart Aloha.

While I was out getting hammered, you were home getting nailed.

I gave her a diamond and she gave me the finger.

If I owed someone an ugly woman and he wouldn't take you, I don't know when I could pay him off.

CHAPTER 100 - SCIENCE

100,000 years ago a space ship full of aliens landed on earth to colonize it.

We ate them.

I try to never be the first guest at a party.

BE WARY OF THE EXTRA WEALTHY

How come the office buildings of the following types always are the biggest and most luxurious?

Bankers

Insurance Companies

Petroleum Companies

Law Offices

Medical Buildings.

Are they cheating us?

SNOTTY CLERKS

Clerk: "Sorry, no refund."

Customer: "But why?"

Clerk: "That's our policy!"

Customer: "Why?"

Clerk: "Sorry, but I don't make the rules around here!"

Customer: "And I'll bet you never will."

HA

BUREAUCRACY

Government employees are so deeply ensconced in their positions that no new regime has ever been able to streamline any part of the good old gravy train.

How about this: Require every member of every treatise on the importance of their department government group to write a one page treatise on the importance of their department. Then send these sheets to other departments for their critique. Could this blow away the chaff?

LIFE'S LESSONS

Starting in about seventh grade we boys are all subject to some kind of shop classes. It wasn't yet science, but it was better than a sand box. We learned to share, play fair, and not hit people. We learned to put things back and clean up your own mess. We learned not to take other's stuff and to say you were sorry if we hurt someone.

Somewhere we learned to wash our hands before we ate, and that warm cookies go great with cold milk.

MAN'S NEEDS

A man can function better if he has the following:

A cook

A house keeper

Daily sex

A child bearer

A child rearer

Companionship

Stimulating conversation.

If he hires all these, every one will be happy.

CHAPTER 101 - EVOLUTON, Dogs and Cats

An essay by Paul Gordon on evolution was refreshingly disingenuous. I imagine that when his father was a boy and was asked to add two apples and two apples, he asked, "What apples?"

Evolution progresses not only by beneficial mutations but also by accommodation to animal practices. For instance, if we domesticate dogs and cats for thousands of years, eventually they are born with an easy adaptability to human association.

After thousands of years of our refining the art of speech, our babies are born with the ability to readily learn to speak.

No one will be born with a "basketball sized brain" because of the limitation to the female bone structure. However, when humans learned to talk, our brain power increased dramatically, thereby causing our heads to expand. That is why the only animal that screams during birthing is the human female.

A Jehovas Wittness asked me, "If you believe in evolution, why don't you go down to the Zoo and watch a monkey turn into a man?"

I answered, "Who's got fifty million years to spend at the Zoo?"

CHAPTER 102 - TAHAA

I once wrote an article on Tahaa, the small island near Raiatea. About 35 years ago, my brother and I, both in our fifties, visited there. A brochure in our Raiatea hotel said it would be a fun boa tride, so we asked about getting there. A guy named Joe took us to his boat which was a canoe with an outboard motor on one side.

The minute we left it started to rain. We spent a half hour in the open ocean, no radio, out of sight of land, but we got there. We were in bathing trunks so Joe asked us if we wanted to dive and see the fish. We tried it, but all I saw down there was a dead cow on the bottom. We then landed on Tahaa and Joe introduced us to the Chief who had lots of teeth missing and many scars from "fighting sharks."

As we strolled down the main drag, we saw one small grocery store and a nice church where a choir was practicing. Joe suggested it was time for the return trip. It rained again on the way back, but stopped just as we beached the canoe.

Joe asked, "How did you like it?"

I replied, "I've had more fun at funerals."

That night at dinner in the hotel, we were joined by another couple, the only other people around. We mentioned that we were born in Davenport, Iowa. The wife in the other couple said, "So was I." Small world!

CHAPTER 103 - HITLER, THE EARLY YEARS

As a boy, Adolph lived in a town in Austria called Deikefrau Ober Essen. In English this would be Fat Wife Over Eating. He applied to attend a local Rabbinical School but for some reason he was rejected. A glimmer of a desire for revenge went through his agile mind.

He had many neighbors to talk to and play with. There was Fur Kakta, Flo Blungent, Hass Ereye, I. Gervaldt, and Fay Schmeer. He liked to talk to the tradespeople in the town's many shops, and especially Doc Sundt, the local Physician. There was Koch Steicker, the butcher, Kake Stacker, the baker, Cohen Holer, the grocer, and I.O. Silver, the banker. He did not like Tuchi Tushi, who was said to be a hooker or Kreis Killer, a sort of loan shark.

He tried selling post cards and then tried painting his own cards, but to no avail. Next he tried painting houses at extremely low bids. But he only painted the front. Then he would ask if they wanted more. That business failed.

Adolph saw his first Chinese when a new restaurant opened in town. When he found out that they could hardly speak Austrian, he knew they were dangerous. Out of fear of the unknown, he visited all the Jewish shop keepers and warned them about the evil Chinese. They all agreed with him, but when he proposed that they wipe them out they hesitated, it might be bad for business.

He told them the reason for the strange taste in Chinese food was because they stole gypsy babies and minced them up in their food after they had gassed them in their ovens. And the tiny ribs they served were baby ribs in every sense. He said that they grew Chinese worms in their basements for the chop suey.

The most important Jew was a man named Bustenhalter, he ran the FAT CHANCE beauty salon. He sold jars of his secret facial formula called "Librarian's Skin." It was made of flour and water. It had various price ranges equivalent to one's social status. He refused to listen to young Hitler, predicting that "he will make trouble some day."

A big war broke out and Adolph enlisted in the German army. He was too frail to be a warrior so they made him a messenger. Sometimes he had to deliver boxes of medals; sometimes he took a few for himself. After the Kaiser surrendered Adolph tried to get a job as a bartender at the Hof Brau Hous ein Munich. They rejected him and he got really angry.

The rest is history.

Johnny Carson's salute to guys like Hitler:

"May your Christmas dinner be a cold can of beans that you eat out in a field and share with a man with one tooth because he owns the spoon."

CHAPTER 104 - AS YE MOW SO SHALL YE REAP

I once bought a 3 horsepower rotary lawn mower at Western Auto supply Co. on their time payment plan.

I started it up in my orchard and began to eagerly roar into the tall grass and weeds that I despised.

It was ravenous as it chewed up and spit out these enemies without regard to flora or fauna. I felt totally empowered and in charge of machine and nature when I noticed I had processed a little lazy lizard.

He [or she] had become chops, ribs and steaks in a micro-second. I paused, resisting a small blasphemy, and in stead uttered an appropriate word of approbation. As I continued my task I was more alert and cautious. I never again caused any reptile dysfunction.

CHAPTER 105 - HOW TO SELL A SCRIPT

When friends read what I write they often say, "You should send that in."

After which I ask, "To whom?" First they look a little frustrated, then they grin and say, "The Readers Digest."

So much for their literary expertise.

Insiders tell me that it is as hard for an unknown to get published as it is for anyone to get an acting job. They hint that talent is secondary to PULL. Writers may slave over a thousand scripts for every one that is made into a movie. Producers seem to prefer to hire a writer on salary. Then they can say, "Write me a script like the one we used last year. It's a safe formula."

I pitched three scripts to 'reputable' script scouts. With no results.

The first was called, "The Last Naked Goddess."

The second was, "The President's Double Murder."

The last was, "The Revenge of the Wet Nurse."

An Action-Hero-Actor read some of my stuff and commented, "I like everything you write. Why aren't you published?"

I replied, "Unless you have a NAME, no one will read it, or maybe I don't need the money that badly."

He said, "Well, if you want to invest, I have some projects."

We all remember how Margaret Mitchell had her "Gone With the Wind" book rejected by thirty publishers before someone bought it. That certainly shows the lack of an efficient screening process on the part of the publishers. I guess it is easier to give your wife's nephew a summer job going through the 'slush' pile of unsolicited manuscripts.

I do feel proud that two scripts I sent in around 1965 were stolen and made into TV series. It proved I was good. A little naïve maybe.

ETHNICITY

In many parts of this world the landlords are of a different ethnicity than the tenants. This can cause problems. Sooner or later all landlords get tired of complaints about every little thing. Some times this means that BIG problems are neglected. When the tenants start associating their disfavor with the ethnicity of the landlord, hate is born.

(no names please)

My wife (Cozy) has an uncle (Karl) who lives in a small European town (Markbriet). One fine day he took a walk with my brother (Lloyd) to show him the sights of their downtown. He stopped and pointed at each of the main buildings and said, "Before WWII all landlords were WEGS (wrong ethnic group), after the war, all WEGS are gone."

This shows that if you are a WEG landlord and skimp a bit on maintenance you will not be popular. It might lead to big trouble and even termination.

Ergo, look for landlords from your own tribe.

THE HOLOCAUST

When Denmark was occupied by the Nazis during the Big War, the Jews were required to wear arm bands so the King wore one, too. The Danes secured the Jews' property and had it all waiting for their return after the war.

The holocaust was a monumental evil as are all genocidal crimes. The racism involved that allowed this to happen was not just with the actual killers, but also with the society from which they came. It was enabled because the killer society preached that the victims were less than human. The colonists of the Americas and also Australia had to believe that the natives were less than human in order to push them aside.

Arabs who sold blacks to slavers did not regard them as human. And how about Vietnam, Cambodia, Bosnia, Armenia, Rwanda, Tibet, Burm , Sudan and the Congo?

WE would never hold prisoners without charges or representation. Right?

CHAPTER 106 - CASEY JONES

Let's not forget the old tunes of the early 1900's

Chorus:

Said Casey Jones just before he died,

"There's two more lines I would like to ride."

The fireman said, "What can they be?"

"They're the Union Pacific and the Sante Fe."

It's a mighty rough road from Lynchville to Danville.

Topped off by a five mile grade.

He was going down grade when he lost his airbrakes,

You should see the mess he made.

He was going down grade hitting 90 miles an hour,

When his whistle broke into a scream.

He was found in the wreck with his hand on the throttle,

He was scalded to death by the steam."

Chorus (alternate)

Said Casey Jones just before he died,

"There's two more women I would like to ride."

The fireman said, "Who can they be.?"

"It's the landlady's daughter and the land ladee."

Wall Street tip: Zeppelin traffic is way down.

DOCTOR OF THE YEAR

The late Dr. Zarver who said, "Your guess is as good as mine."

Note: After he was hospitalized for chest pains, the staff was unaware he had died.

CHAPTER 107 - RIGHTEOUSNESS

We may not have peace and prosperity, but we have RIGHTEOUSNESS.

The only thing we have to fear is fear itself, plus toxic water, toxic waste, ozone depletion, the green house effect, earth quakes, wild fires, terrorists, termites, and old age. But we have federal righteousness.

Clinton gave us peace, prosperity, and sex. The Republicans gave us recession, war, and righteousness.

RETIREMENT

There is a perfect place for you to retire. It is only $4200 a month plus utilities.

An African King hid his throne in a grass shack to protect it from thieves. But it burned down. People who live in grass houses shouldn't stow thrones.

If it's not broken, you don't have kids.

Even bad people are biodegradable.

Don't you wish that during the Olympics, the winners would give speeches to thank all the people they could think of?

Some one should sell plastic coffins, they would last a lot longer than wood.

"Ve muss save money vor taxes, ve muss combine the two offices of Mayor undt Villiage Idiot" [from the long lost papers of Hans, Einstein's gardener]

We thought life was a cabaret, but there seems to be a two drink minimum.

Rats in a lab got cancer from sun tan lotion. Later it was found that rats in a lab get cancer from everything.

CHAPTER 108 – EMOTIONS

People who have control of their emotions find it very useful. If you really lose your temper, others will think less of you, but if it's a case where you really need to win a point against someone, pretending to lose your temper will often win out. If someone thinks you are very mad they will try to settle the problem in a hurry. It works.

Raising your voice in a store or a restaurant will usually bring you instant consideration.

A lot of women know how to fake affection, some for fun, some for profit.

You can fake interest in someone or even fake stupidity when it serves you.

Some fake happiness or sadness. It takes practice

Faking interest in a wallflower can improve a life.

BRAINS

The brain has a mind of its own. It wants to have fun; it wants to feel good whatever the consequences. Many an addict has left a rehab place confident that they will never use that

BAD stuff again. But the pleasure seeking part of the brain can have other ideas and it can turn the car or taxi right around and head straight for the place where one obtains the BAD stuff.

SIN

Sin is an idea invented by clergy who wanted power and control. Sin is part of the dogma (ground rules) of some religions. BUT HOW CAN YOU SIN IF YOU DON'T BELIEVE IN SIN? Some Bible beaters scream that "you were conceived in sin!"

Children must be fed their parents' dogma at an early age where they will believe anything an adult tells them, otherwise it will bring up more questions than faith. The dictionary says "Faith is the belief in something for which there is no proof. And, all religions were invented by unsophisticated men who thought the earth was flat and the center of the universe.

So people who don't buy the Sin Theory never sin.

CHAPTER 109 - GRAFT

If a politician can be named to the 'Graft' Committee he is sure of reelection. What if our lawmakers were paid a salary equal to an average of their 'reported' income to the IRS for the last five years?

WE the PEOPLE keep these guys in office, but they sneer at us behind our backs. They say, "You can't fool the American voters!" They do it all the time. We elect actors, muscle men, and rich men's sons. Just so long as they are good looking and can read their lines.

LEADER OF THE FREE WORLD

Freedom loving people of the world look to our President for leadership,

until we bomb them.

If our Pres. cannot pronounce the name of the country we are going to invade, or if our Generals can't find it on a map, maybe we should ask the United Nations to do the invading

A day without sunshine is like night.

CHAPTER 110 - POETRY HAS RULES

Poems consist of verses. Verses rhyme. Like "I saw a cat, It wore a hat," Is that so difficult?

Just because you type your stupid ideas on just the left side of the page doesn't make it more profound and it is NOT a poem (in my op.)

Why read it if it doesn't rhyme, and preferably it should have a cadence or meter. Like Iambic Pentameter. It is a hundred times more difficult, but in the end, people will enjoy it. And convolutions of sentences, just to put the rhyming word on the end, defeat the whole effect.

Look at the beautiful simplicity of 'Trees" by Kilmer.

I think that I shall never see,

A poem lovely as a tree.

A tree that looks at God all day,

And lifts its leafy arms to pray,

A tree that may in summer wear,

A nest of robins in her hair.

    Etc.

It's like a friendly conversation in perfect meter and just happens to rhyme. Maybe if Kilmer had just typed it on the left side of the page, he could have saved himself a lot of thinking time.

Take that old guy Geoffrey Chaucer back in the 1300s; even though sometimes imprisoned by the French, he could write poetry that influenced his language. In his Canterbury Tales, he glides with such ease we don't mind if his words are a bit obscure today.

In that Aprille with the shores sotte,

The draught of March has pierced to the roote,   (some re spelled)

If he could do the rhyme and rhythm schtick 700 years ago with a goose quill and a bottle of home made ink, well, think about what a lead pencil could have done for him. It would have been 'high tech.'

QUIPS

Drunk, "I'd like to apply for the job of fathering your children,"

Drag Queen, "Sorry, but I don't have an opening."

Two well dressed ladies were walking across the church lawn after services. One exclaimed to the other, "Oh shit, I stepped on some doggie dew."

Foreign car boast, "It will last as long as a land mine."

Wives have the right to remain silent, but some are not up to the job.

Men are dumb and women are nuts.

If you reach the age of 65 you are legally old.

Note: When using your lap-top as you drive to work, if you foolishly light up a cigarette the second hand smoke will infiltrate your computer chips and send cancer cells throughout your E-mail. Safeguard your loved one (your steno?) as she tries to transcribe your shit.

TweNty years from now all Doctors and Engineers will be Middle Easternasian.

CHAPTER 111 - ENGLISHMEN

Standing on a London street corner, waiting to cross, an English friend next to me said, "London has a very high auto accident rate."

I replied, "No wonder, they all drive on the wrong side of the street."

He objected, "Oh I'd say the shoe was on the other foot, rah-thur."

I was talking about traffic and he was talking about shoes.

Later, I said to this friend, "The trouble with you English is, first you borrow

Our language and then you louse it up."

He snorted, "Oh I don't know you know don't you know?"

He had me there.

I posed a question to this gentleman. Suppose you had a wife and six daughters in a cabin on an American prairie and were surrounded by a thousand savage Indians…and you had three carrier pigeons you could send for help, one to a British Army, one to a German Army, or one to the U.S. Cavalry. Which would you choose?"

He thought for a moment then said, "I guess I'd pick the German Army."

That says a lot about a country that said the withdrawal from Dunkirk was a victory.

CHAPTER 112 - OUTSOURCING IS OUT OF CONTROL

Can outsourcing run out of sources? Follow the money. Our Asian friends would be happy to take over the jobs of our lawmakers and for a pittance of pay. Our fat cat corporate chairmen and their board of director buddies can award themselves hundreds of millions of dollars in bonuses and who's to stop them? The stockholders? If he's small he'll be ignored, if he's big he'll be bought. Out sourcing doesn't help We The People. It helps cut corporate costs and contributes to the cash cows, and, oh yes, it helps the man learning English-by-phone in Pakistan who has a wife and twelve children.

BONUS BABIES

Some towns in Italy now pay bonuses to families that have babies, while China had a rule of limiting each family to one child. Spain, meanwhile, has a birth rate too low to maintain its population. American minorities are breeding themselves into majorities. The rich have found that they can get richer by paying low wages and keeping the borders open. We have a choice; vote the rich out of office or learn Spanish. If we paid what a job is worth, maybe our fine citizens on welfare would take jobs.

SOCIAL SECURITY

These funds are so tempting to a greedy congress. But where are they? Let's see, Pres. Johnson used the numbers to make the deficit look smaller, then Reagan put the dough in

241

the general fund to make HIS deficits look smaller. Today, the S.S. payments to people come out of the general fund, which will always be there. so how can the system go broke?

DEFICITS

Some say that the way to reduce deficits during a war is to reduce the government's income. If this is true we should try it on our family budgets.

Maybe we could get the president to stand on an aircraft carrier and announce that the deficit is GONE.

ATOMIC ENERGY INCENTIVES

The nuclear energy expert Edward Teller once said that if you pitched a tent alongside a nuclear power plant you would get as much radiation as if your neighbor across the street had had a tooth ex-rayed.

When nuke energy was first designed it was calculated that it would make electricity so cheap that there would be no use sending out bills.

Then various non-scientific groups started demanding more and more safe guards until now it costs almost as much as coal-fired electricity. (yippee). Maybe we should start building nuclear power plants again. Maybe we need a government incentive plan.

Remember, no person in this country, with all our safeguards, has ever so much as torn a finger nail in our nuclear power plants. Over 50 years?

RACES RACISTS

No one knows the skin color of the Africans of 100,000 years ago.

Disirregardless (not a real word) they were our ancestors

INTERPERSONAL EVALUATIONS

If you want to know how you stand in someone else's eyes, go to their house and say, "Hey, can I have an ashtray?"

CHAPTER 113 - TIMES CHANGE

Pity the poor music teacher; no one seems to take lessons any more.

TITLEISTS

Some people are addicted to their titles. Doctors seem to be the biggest advocates of getting their title mentioned every few minutes. Every time a doctor calls me by my first name, I make sure that I know HIS first name.

Others have titles that they believe are just as prestigious. Like doctors of the rocket and aerospace sciences, captains, maestros, deans, coaches, managers, CEOs, company presidents, military officers, maitre d's [short for master of the hotel], lady, dame, hooker, etc.

PROFESSIONS

In the first lecture session in Engineering College they advise you: "Take a good look at the person on your right and on your left. Next year there will only be one of you left. But be nice to the drop-outs, some day they will be your lawyers and doctors.

FALLING OAKS

If a tree falls in the forest, it makes the same kind of air vibrations as a symphony orchestra playing chop sticks. Vibrations are not sound, just movements of the air. Sound is produced inside your brain when the air vibrations tickle your ear drums. Then they are transmitted to other tiny parts that send an electrical signal to your brain, if any.

INSULTS TO BE SAVED UNTIL NEEDED

Here's a dollar, buy a condom so you don't reproduce yourself.

You would be out of your depth in a parking lot puddle.

You have delusions of adequacy.

If you would shut your mouth you would bite your foot..

I can't believe you beat out a million other sperm.

You are depriving some village of their idiot.

Your I.Q. is steady, right at room temperature.

If they start taxing brain power, you'll get a refund.

I can see the wheels turning in your head, but the hamster is dead.

.

Store clerk: "Hey, I don't make the rules here."

Customer: "And I'm sure you never will."

OFFICES

Some people wonder why the offices of some businesses are so splendiferous, and luxurious. Particularly banks, insurance offices, oil companies, law and medicine. Don't complain, if they knew what they were doing they would double their fees and prices.

INVADERS

100,000 years ago a space craft full of aliens landed on earth to colonize us. We ate them. Maybe they could have arrived at a more convenient time.

DROP OUTS

Every school drop-out makes a conscious decision to be uneducated for the rest of his life. Their response = Sooo ?

BASQUES

These nice people live mostly near the border between France and Spain. When they build a new house, they always make sure to have several outside doors. They don't want to have all their Basques in one exit.

CHAPTER 114 - DOPE

The WAR AGAINST DRUGS SOLUTION [WADS]

We've spent zillions on our war against illegal drugs. Some say that the costs of the enforcement would go to zero if we legalized everything. Sure.

Our enforcement seems to have stayed away from the foreign suppliers and the local users. Most of our efforts have been against the dealers, distributors, wholesalers, and cross-border trafficking. These methods don't seem to get the job done so maybe a new idea is needed.

More jail time seems unpopular since our prisons are over stuft.

MAYBE IF YOU FINED THE USERS ENOUGH THE MARKET WOULD DRY UP. As long as there is a buyer someone will sell it.

If a user [casual, social, addict etc.] was fined $5000 for a first time conviction and if upon a subsequent conviction a ZERO WAS ADDED TO THE FINE, it would take the fun out of snorting, smoking, shooting up, and pill popping.

But, you say, what about the unemployed, the unemployable, the poor, the lifelong addicts on welfare, the handicapped [physically or mentally] the homeless and the hopeless? We could provide state or city street maintenance and similar jobs at minimum wages to pay off their fines.

Any such culprits holding green cards, student and tourist visas, so called "legal residents' and those holding naturalization papers should be deported. AND, they would be allowed no future entry to U.S., Canada, or Mexico.

HOWEVER, experience shows that the congressional negotiations over the wording of such legislation could take a hundred years

CHAPTER 115 - SCIENCE EDUCATION INCENTIVES

My Engineering college had only two foreign students that I knew of, they were from the middle east, Turkey. I think their names were Morataglu and Moratzad. When they arrived in the solid green of our middle west, one remarked, "Allah must be here, not back there in the sand." They bought a used car but soon wrecked it because of the temptation of long straight roads.

Today our science classes have about fifty percent foreign students. OUR obese boys and over weight girls would rather take any easy set of courses that will provide a degree, any degree. Then when their families cut off their funding and the job market is zero for their particular 'skills' they decide life is unfair. They hate their parents and their supervisor at McDonalds and end up in protest marches, against anything.

Our society would benefit if scientists were held up to as high esteem as rock singers or TV detectives.

Students taking Liberal Arts and making good grades should be bribed to switch to science.

A 'will' is a dead giveaway.

When a girl gets married she gets a new name and a dress.

CHAPTER 116 - HE HAS A BOMB

Like potato chips, you can't have just one atom bomb. Even a few, along with their delivery rockets, are worse than none. If you should decide to use them — then they are gone, and now here comes the retaliation — bang! 'Alles kaput'.

If you just have them around to brag about, then you become a likely target when some nukes mysteriously arrive on someone who has a lot of them, it is too late to say, "I didn't do it." Your land is gone. No matter how you scream about nuclear proliferation, sooner or later, there will be doom's day bombs in unstable hands. Then, 'hands across the sea' has a whole new meaning.

For fifty years the Big Boys have had stock piles that assured their own destruction if ever used. But the little guy, with just a few, is a sitting duck.

VISA

Most of the world would like to move to the U.S. and be rich like us. There are three ways to do this.

1. Wait on your country's quota until your turn comes up.

2. Sneak across our border and pretend you were born here.

3. Apply for a tourist or student visa for a specified period of time, and   then ignore your promise to follow the rules about leaving and stay and prosper or go on welfare. No one from the Immigration Dept, will ever come looking for you. It's not in their budget or job description.

 Some tourists and students have been here for fifty years. Who needs fences on the border? Nothing will change as long as the Fat Cats need cheap labor.

We are all in shape. Round is a shape.

CHAPTER 117 - LEAF RAKING

HOW TO CLOSE MILITARY BASES

In the Great Depression the government hired the unemployed to rake leaves and other 'odd' jobs to boost the economy. It put money into circulation. Many of our military bases no longer provide any strategic purpose except to provide jobs for a senator or congressman's voters.

Every so often the military brass is told by congress to close unnecessary bases so as to reduce the defense budget. Then the hue and cry goes up, "Not this base, it's important." Yada yada yada.

The biggest part of the U.S. budget goes to the Defense [WAR] Department so it's a fair target for cuts. And if you ask how many military bases, installations, or offices there are, you run into definitions galore. Nobody knows.

In Peacetime, the next time we have a PEACE TIME, here is a simple suggestion on how to erase half the bases. I said SIMPLE so it will be labeled 'over simplified.' Send a one page request to the Head Honcho, Stud Duck, Leader of each military 'place' and ask for a one page reply stating how they could reduce their expenses by 50% if ordered to.

A few simple ground rules might be listed such as: In reducing the ranks of men and women in uniform, all ranks need to be reduced equally (We have over 850 generals). Some real estate leases might need to be broken, some equipment might have to be abandoned. Keep it simple, stupid [kiss].

Can't you just hear the uproar, "Not in MY backyard [NIMBY]

Note : We may be short of troops but we have over 850 generals.

As Allen Sherman used to sing: "Do not make a stingy sandwich, pile the cold cuts high, customers should see salami, coming through the rye."

"If I'd shot you when I wanted to, I'd be outta jail by now.

Beauty is in the eye of the beer holder.

CHAPTER 118 - RED, WHITE AND BLUE

Some of my friends are Red, White and Blue:

Red Neck, White Trash, and Blue Collar

HEALTH

The health nuts are going to feel really stupid some day when they are in a hospital dying of nothing.

EVIDENCE

If Supreme Court were asked to judge the truth of the Bible, what would it use for evidence?

ENGINEERING

Everything you own that either has batteries or that plugs in, is beyond the scope of most people. Therefore, the entertainment industry does not exploit Engineers like it does the other three professions.

THANKS

Israel helped us so much in the Gulf War and the Iraqi War that we should thank them by sending them 3 million dollars a day. (We do?)

BIG PROFITS

We have a 60 billion dollar a month trade deficit with Asia...

This is allowed to go on because our guys who are getting rich off of these imports are big political contributors

.

WHO KILLED THE POPE?

When we were in Rome in 1978 the town was buzzing because the Pope, who only had the job for a month, had died. The word on the street and in the bars was that he had been murdered because of his new ideas. Nothing could be done about it because the Vatican is an independent country

BLACK HOLES

A Black Hole in outer space is a place where the gravity is so strong that light cannot shine or escape. This make a kind of sense when you consider that the center of an atom is always about 1830 times heavier than the electrons going around it.. They say that the center is made up of stuff they call quarks and gluons, whatever, but if you had a bit of that nucleus the size of a sugar cube, just nuclei, alone, it would weigh 14,000 tons. It would go right down through the earth an d out the other side, I guess.

That must be the stuff that makes the Black Holes so strong.

AN OLD GEEZER

He said he was "Home Immunized" because he had exposed himself to every bad germ there was.

LIFE

Life is not SO precious that it must be preserved at ALL costs.

LAS VEGAS

What happens in Vegas stays in Vegas and the money bet in Vegas stays in Vegas..

DEFENSE

Today, the President, who declined to be identified, said, "Defense can stop an emergency but disarmament can't."

SCHOOL BOARDS

Our school boards that are against the 'theory' of evolution are probably also opposed to the theory of algebra, history, geography and arithmetic.

BLISS

If 'ignorance is bliss' the world should be happy.

CHAPTER 119 - PASTIES

Rule of thumb for gals: If it has tires or testicles you will have trouble with it.

Rule for men: No matter how pretty she is, some other guy is sick of putting up with her crap.

There oughta be a law against blind people sky diving. It scares the shit out of the dog.

Trailer Parks attract tornados.

Israel is building a 380 mile fence against terrorism. I wish we could afford to do that.

Airlines resist spending millions for terrorist's missile defense. After all, if they get shot down they can say it was NOT their fault.

Once there were two Irishmen. Both were named Patty. One was Patty O'Toole and the other was Patty O'Furniture.

Wife: I need 2000 dollars for a boob job.

Husband: Just rub some toilet paper between your boobs and they will get big.

Wife: That will never
work.

Husband: It worked on
your ass.

MISSIONARIES

Two missionaries were in the dark jungle at midnight surrounded by natives. One said, "I don't like the sound of those drums."

A voice from the jungle said, "He's not our regular drummer."

TAXES

True Story: An accountant was helping an elderly couple do their taxes. He asked, "And how much did you give to the church?"

The old lady said, "Oh, what's that quarter on Easter."

GUN CONTROL

Taiwan passed a law making a death sentence mandatory for any gun possession. The crime rate went way down but their National Riflemakers Association disbanded in protest.

SENIORS

The Doctor said to the old man, "I'll need urine, blood and stool samples."

The old man asked his wife, "What did he say?"

She said, "He wants your shorts,"

A MURDER DEFENSE

A Texas politician promised to spend more, tax less, and balance the budget. So someone shot him. The man was acquitted because of his defense, "He needed killin'."

MAD DOGS

We don't shoot mad dogs to teach other dogs not to become rabid. We do it to get them off the streets.

SNOW

He wanted to be a snob but he found it very difficult to find someone to be superior to.

COLLEGE

If you belong in college you will be smart enough to find a way to get there.

And it takes a lot of practice to be able to judge a book by its cover.

ARITHMETIC

A flight crew decided to fly around the world at forty thousand feet... They actually flew it at 40,001 feet. How much longer did that make the trip?

You can solve this in your head if you remember that Circumference = Pi times the diameter.

If twenty divided by two is ten how much is twenty divided by .5 ? (That was point five)

CHAPTER 120 - OLDE FUNDAMENTALS

The famous writer of swashbuckler novels, Raphael Sabatine, wrote a couple of lines that are worth remembering.

1. He said, "Life is one long succession of making the best of second choices."
2. Once in one of his novels, a handsome young guard was assigned to be a body guard for the princess when she took her daily ride. She asked him, "What would you do if I were not a princess?" He replied, "In all this idle world there is nothing quite so idle as imagining that which we would do if things were different."

MENTALISTS

Most modern fundamentalists are not qualified to understand the marvelous metaphors of the world's religions.

GUNS DON'T DIE, PEOPLE DO

In 1983 the Supreme Court reaffirmed the right of the states and cities to regulate or ban firearms.

A new handgun is manufactured every 13 seconds.

Every two and one half minutes a handgun is used to shoot someone.

We now have he ability to put little serial numbers on every bullet. The National Riflemakers Association is fighting a law to require this on all ammo. They say it would interfere with hunting.

Hunting with machine guns should be banned.

FAITH IN HORSE SENSE

Substituting religion for education has been tried for a thousand years. It doesn't work.

CHAPTER 121 - KEEP IT SIMPLE

Dear Editor: 10-12-04

I remember President Hoover's run for reelection. Before the advent of televised presidential debates we only had 'stump' speeches and very few of us got to see the man in person.. Hoover returned to the place of his birth, West Branch, Iowa, to make an important speech in his unsuccessful bid for reelection. I was a senior in Davenport High School and too young to vote. A buddy of mine and I borrowed a Model A Ford and drove the sixty miles to West Branch. There were crowds of people, Iowa and Illinois State Police and a huge circus tent that was erected for his speech. We squeezed in through the throngs of eager Republicans and listened to his oration.

Hoover was an Engineer, graduated from Stanford and knew his job very well. He spoke of tariffs and international consortiums and I discovered that 1 could hardly understand a word. In fact I was most impressed by the Indian motorcycles used by the Illinois State Police. I saw they had a small four cylinder in-line engine that sounded like a sewing machine when it was idling. We drove home and announced that we had seen the big man.

Much later it dawned on me that he and others after him had lost the ear of the average voter because of their use of big words and flowery phrases. Carter seemed more down to earth than Ford. Reagan spoke more to the common man than Carter. Clinton was easier to follow than Bush the elder, and his son was more common-place than Gore. I guess debates should appeal to our understanding.

Sincerely, Baron Von Schnedkloth

CHAPTER 122 - RELIGION RECIPROCOLS

Persons who want to share their religious views with you almost never want you to share yours with them.

If you think a person is very nice but then you notice they are rude to the waiter, you can realize that they are only being nice to you for a reason, like , they want something from you. When they get around to giving you their `pitch', give them a quarter and tell them to call someone who cares.

I am like fine wine. I started out like a nice ripe grape. Then I met my wife and she stomped the shit out of me until I became something acceptable to have dinner with. But I still dangle participles?

There is more money being spent on breast implants and Viagra than on Alzheimer's research. By the time we get into an "assisted living" home, everyone will have perky boobs and big erections and no recollections of what to do with them.

In a recent survey it was found that everybody is an above average driver.

About 8258 years ago [plus or minus 10,000 years] a guy named Noah was supposed to have built a boat big enough to have held a mating pair of every animal, bird, insect, lizard, amphibian,, snake etc. on earth with food and water for forty days. The craft was probably about a mile long and square ended. Then around 1914 a fine group of British Engineers and Naval Architects built a perfect ship called the TITANIC.

QUESTION: Which one sank on it's first trip?

Before you answer, remember that Noah had no iron or steel, no saws, no nails, drills, no glue, no knives, just a bunch of stone hammers made of flint. Also, some of the South American tree sloth move so slowly that if they went to answer the call to go to the Middle East, they would not be there yet.

ANSWER: As to the above question, both boats sank. Lloyd's of London had them both insured.

NEWS FLASH

According to the latest astronomical spectroscopic analysis, all the elements needed for the evolution of life are out there in space. If needed.

Some people work hard and get rich. Some lay back and believe they're 'cool.' But the latter think they are entitled to the same goodies as the former. Every one is entitled to go to Beverly Hills High School. All they have to do is move to Beverly Hills. Simple.

Thousands of teen aged girls have become pregnant without having sex. They say, "But Mother, we didn't do it!" Maybe she didn't, but her boyfriend did. Human spermatozoa are eager to travel right through any underpants she is wearing. No problem.

"Mother, I did not!"

The problem has been around since underpants were invented. Maybe 2005 years ago.

I remember a lady in charge of a girl's college dormitory [matron, chaperone, duane] caused quite a stir of laughter seventy years ago by suggesting that young ladies take along a magazine on a double date, to cover a boy's lap, in the event she is required to sit on such a lap. This advice was told and retold to every one's amusement.

HOWEVER, the lady was probably right. What with light summer dresses, horny boys, and bouncing cars, this Friday Night Fever was probably fatal to faithful feminine fidelity, virginity not withstanding.

Any magazine could stop that which summer fabric could not. The Madame Dufarge of the dormitory might have been overly righteous — but she was right. Right?

CHAPTER 123 - DEAR MR. POPE

Dear Mr. Pope, Your Grace, Hope and Charity, Sir:

I'm new at this and I need a little help trying to live up to all the things that God wrote in His book. If you can't answer these questions about the Bible maybe you could ask the Author, I'm told you speak to him regularly.

When I burn a bull on the altar as a sacrifice, I know it creates a pleasing odor for the Lord [lev.1:9]. The problem is my neighbors. They claim the odor is not pleasing to them. Should I smite them?

I would like to sell my daughter into slavery, as sanctioned in Exodus 21:7. In this day and age, what do you think would be a fair price for her?

I know that I am allowed no contact with a woman while she is in her period of menstrual uncleanliness [Lev.15:19-24]. The problem is, how do I tell? I have tried asking, but most women take offense.

Lev. 25:44 states that I may indeed possess slaves, both male and female, provided they are purchased from neighboring nations. A friend of mine claims that this applies to Mexicans, but not Canadians. Can you clarify? Why can't I own Canadians?

I have a neighbor who insists on working on the Sabbath. Exodus 35:2 clearly states he should be put to death. Am I morally obligated to kill him myself?

A friend of mine feels that even though eating shellfish is an abomination [Lev, 11:10], it is a lesser abomination than homosexuality. I don't agree. Can you settle this?

Lev. 21:20 states that I may not approach the altar of God if I have a defect in my sight. I have to admit that I wear reading glasses. Does my vision have to be 20/20, or is there some wiggle room here?

Most of my male friends get their hair trimmed, including the hair around their temples, even though this is expressly forbidden by Lev. 19:27. How should they die?

I know from Lev. 11:6-8 that touching the skin of a dead pig makes me unclean, but may I still play football if I wear gloves?

My uncle has a farm. He violates Lev. 19:19 by planting two different crops in the same field, as does his wife by wearing garments made of two different kinds of thread (cotton/polyester blend). He also tends to curse and blaspheme a lot. Is it really necessary that we go to all the trouble of getting the whole town together to stone them [Lev. 14:10-16]? Couldn't we just burn them to death at a private family affair like we do with people who sleep with their in-laws? [Lev. 20:14]

I know you have studied these things extensively, so I am confident you can help. Thank you again for reminding us that God's word is eternal and unchanging.

CHAPTER 124 - THE HEAD MAN

Gladys Peters hated her name. Those mean boys in her ninth grade class called her, "Glad-ass Pee-turds." So she told her friends to call her TANYA and they agreed. She liked to sail her tiny dory (the Hunky Dory) out onto Lake Michigan, but her parents restricted her to the marina area. Except on Sunday morning when they slept 'til noon. Then Tanya would sail way out. She had become quite adept at sailing and in any breeze she could do figure eights. She was good.

This early Sunday she decided to get out of sight of land. Well, maybe just to where you could still see the last little bit of shore on the horizon. She took along her favorite sandwich, peanut butter with frills, a jug of water and some sun screen. She pronounced, as she sailed away, "I may be only fourteen, but I'm not stupid."

She kept sailing at a steady pace until she could barely see any of the shoreline. She remarked, "The lake is as calm as a cucumber; I could sail all the way to Alaska." She squinted at something on the surface in the distance. It looked a bit like an aberrant beach ball.

As she turned the rudder she mused, "What's that in the water ahead, a head?" The closer she got the more it did look like a head. Finally, she was positive. She steered the boat alongside, dropped the sail; and addressed the floating head, "Ahoy there. You must be some swimmer, way out here."

The head said, "I cannot swim."

"Is there more to you or are you just a head?"

"Don't be stupid."

"How did you get way out here, did your boat sink? Or are you standing on a submarine."

"I am on a secret mission."

"How long? You have no food or water."

"I have plenty of water, but no food for two or three days, I forgot."

"Would you like some of my sandwich/"

"What kind?"

"Its my fave, peanut butter with added peanuts on top, and just a lil slop of jelly. Here, I'll get it out and you can try it." She puts an end of the sandwich in his mouth and he chews ravenously.

"That is excellent. What do you call that?"

"Super Schrunchy. Want some more?"

"Yes, please. That would be complimented by green Chilean wine. But this lake water will do." She feeds him more.

'No foolin,' besides the secret mission, what're you really doing out here?"

"Promise not to tell?"

"I threw away the key."

"So sorry. I'm waiting here for a boatload of whores. Then I push the trigger and blow those sinning infidels to perdition."

"That's suicide."

"If they do not come by sundown, my brothers will pick me up and reposition me."

She pondered, "The only lake traffic here is the ore boats from the Mesabi Iron Range."

"That is it, the "ore" boat."

"It won't hurt the U.S. much if you sink a boat full of 'ore'"

"Why not?"

"We have enough for a thousand years."

"Aha, and then what?"

"We'll probably switch to titanium."

"It is rare?"

"My geologist boy friend says it's the sixth most abundant stuff on earth."

"I think we make mistake."

"Looks like you're the goat."

"I have many goats, you mean my 'brothers' are wasting our lives?"

"I would take you home with me but you must be wearing some kind of bomb. Right?"

"Fifty kilos of TNT."

"You got a detonator thingy?"

"Right in my hand."

"Well, its been nice, gotta go, don't be a stranger, or drop in if you, oh well." She put the small mast in its socket and the sail began to fill. As she grabbed the tiller she shouted, "When your rat-faced friends come at sundown, why don't you pull the trigger, teach them a lesson they'll never forget. I'll be sitting on the porch, hoping to hear from you," From a distance, she waved. "Now he looks so sad."

As she watched the sun sink in the west, she was greeted with a distant blast of water and boat parts, a bit like distant thunder. She smiled and said, "There he goes, a head of his time."

CHAPTER 125 - THE HOLIDAY PLANET

(or, Tom Swift and his electric light bill)

Flash Gordon Fogelman was approaching the Holiday Inn resort planet in his tritanium rocket ship. How he loved that ship, he even called it, "Her." He hurried through customs and security and found himself in tall hall where there was a vast array of adventure selections available for rent. Each scenario put you in a false environs where you could disport in your secret delusion.

Tourists such as Flash were called PATSYS (Playing as they steal your shirt) and they had no inkling as to the dangers they would meet. After a long self debate, Flash chose "The Wild West, Save a Fair Maiden." He paid his money and was ushered into a big black booth.

At once, he was in a vast western vista with purple mountain majesties above the cactus plain. Nearby was a talking saddle horse who said, "I'm Daisy." She winked at him and purred as he mounted her.

They followed the broad banks of a babbling brook full of threshing trout and spawning salmon until a ranch house loomed like a lump of logs on the horizon. He was approaching

275

the rear yard of the homesteaded hacienda when he thought he heard a faint female scream for help. Goading Daisy into a gallop he saw wild Indians dancing around someone on the lawn.

He whipped out his six-shooter and fired six shots into the air. The cowardly braves bolted into the bushes and disappeared. He dismounted to creep closer, reloading his empty gun as he went, wondering what the dirty dancing had been about. He hopped a hedge and hove to at the sight of a naked young girl, tied to stakes and spread eagled on the lawn.

She whimpered and said, "Oh, thank you, thank you for saving me, don't look at me, those horrible savages stacked us, stole our horses and live stock, don't look at me, and if you hadn't come along, I don't know what they would have done, ravish, I guess, whatever that is, don't look at me, I'm only sixteen."

As he started to unbutton the front of his pants he said, "This just isn't your day."

At that electrified moment an elderly feminine voice from the cabin said firmly, "Time to come in Kathy, play time is over." The girl rolled over, pulled up the stakes, gathered up her clothes and tromped off towards the house. He faintly heard the word, "Shit."

The western scene faded and he was back in the big black booth. A robotic voice said, "Your adventure is over. Please proceed to the lobby to make your next selection." He mumbled something that sounded like, "Shit."

CHAPTER 126 - THE CARE, CLEANING AND CLAIMING OF TRAVELER'S CHECKS

I recently returned from my 50th college reunion. I was the oldest attendee, which probably means I am in the springtime of my senility. Before I left home I had grabbed a plastic folder with some old traveler's checks from previous vacations and stuffed them into a camera case. It was a tiring trip and when I returned home I put on my friendly old terry cloth robe. I took the checks out of the camera case and slipped them into my robe pocket, planning to hide them from my wife the next day.

She usually gets up about three hours earlier than I do, so when I appeared the next morning she handed me the plastic traveler's check folder and asked, "What's this? I washed your robe and this must have been in the pocket."

I said, "Where is the $400?"

She said, "What?" Then she rushed to search the washer and dryer and came back with just a handful of confetti. She demanded, "Why would you—?

I demanded, "Why did you—?"

Now the house was like a library. The only sound was from the gears in my twenty-two clocks. I read the whole L.A. Times, even including my horoscope, which said, "Be careful with money."

Finally, I got our my camera case, unloaded my video camera and its accessories, and found a lot of old receipts that covered the bottom of the case like a bird cage. There was a receipt for ten Thomas Cook traveler's checks at $50 each. I called the 800 number given and some lady named Karen was very cordial.

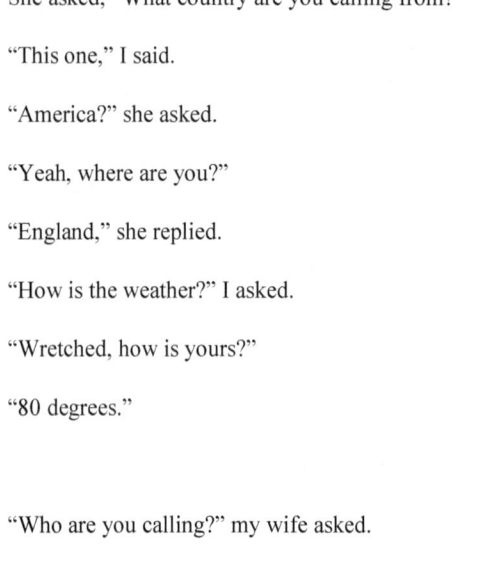

She asked, "What country are you calling from?"

"This one," I said.

"America?" she asked.

"Yeah, where are you?"

"England," she replied.

"How is the weather?" I asked.

"Wretched, how is yours?"

"80 degrees."

"Who are you calling?" my wife asked.

"England," I replied.

She gave me such a look.

On the phone, My Fair Lady took down all the data and said, "You cashed one in Guadalajara (pronounced with a 'jar'). Any since then?"

I replied, "Yes, one on a Mississippi River gambling boat."

"Do they still have those?" she wondered. "Sir, do you know of a place called Burbank?" She then gave me directions to a Burbank bank. I went there, they called the Fair Lady, and I got new checks.

I guess the lesson is that the receipts are more valuable than the checks. Don't let them get wet. I think they are designed to dissolve, and money laundering is a No No. Now my wife and I are speaking again.

CHAPTER 127 - SOME 50 YEAR OLD JOKES

A man walked into a bar carrying a small dog. He said to the barkeep, "If my dog talks for you will you give us a free drink?'

The bar man said, "Get outta here."

The man said to the dog, "Fido, what's that up there?'

The dog said, "Roof."

Then the man said, "Fido, how's business?"

The dog said, "Rough."

The man said, "Fido, who was the greatest baseball player there every was?"

The dog said, "Ruth."

The barman said, "Get out now or I will throw you out!"

As the man was walking out the door, the little dog looked back over the man's shoulder and asked, "Dimaggio?"

Gentleman to Lady, "How come you don't have any breasts?"

She replied, "Get off my back, George."

At The Last Supper, Jesus turned to his disciples and said, "You'll all have to get on this side of the table if you want to get in the picture."

Lawyer to rape victim, "Did he say anything before he raped you?"

Girl: "It was too awful to repeat."

Judge: "Would you just write it down on this piece of paper so we can show it to the jury.

She wrote the sentence: "I'm gonna fuck you to death."

As the piece of paper was passed from juror to juror, one man was asleep.

The lady next to him poked him in the ribs until he awoke and then passed him the note. He read it and put it into his inside coat pocket.

The judge said: "Sir, will you pass the note along to the other jurors?'

The man said: "No, it's personal."

NEW JOKE

Oprah is Harpo spelled backwards. Maybe she could learn something from him.

IF

If our politicians can't find a place on the map, don't send our troops there.

CHAPTER 128 - THE TWELFTH KNIGHT

The kind ordered his twelve sons, all knights, to assemble on the first of the next month to attend his annual briefing on future affairs. This momentous event always evoked a pissing contest among the boys for points and prestige.

The twelfth and youngest son was by far the most ambitious. Any of the boys would gladly use their swords to decapitate the wicked ruler if it meant they could be crowned King, but number twelve was the only one actually making plans for such an assassination. He had three plans: Plan A assumed that a big bold move such as lopping off the King's head would put his brothers in such awe of his bravery that they would crown him the new King. Plan B involved killing all of his eleven brothers. However, this seemed to be full of peril, pitfalls, and a pratfall or two.

Plan C had vague, dreamy possibilities. Last season he had sent a short epistle to the very rich Virgin Queen of Prussia, asking for an audience. A favorable reply would permit a courtship, and if that courtship resulted in a marriage, he was sure to be picked by his oppressive papa to be the Heir Apparent Crown Prince. Papa's parental pride would be piqued by the prospect of his pairing up with the pretty Empress of Prussia, of whom there were none richer.

However, unless she answered his fervent but formal request for a rendezvous, Plan C was just an impossible dream. Plan A still seemed to be the best way to go.

The only time the Knight sons could even get near the King was during one of these annual briefings. The security precautions of the evil ruler were bold and bizarre. Before the meeting, each son had to be disarmed, stripped naked by an old witch, and clad in a long slip-over robe that would only fit a nine foot giant. Sitting on a stool, so attired, no son could rush the King without tripping over the skirts of his robe.

In anticipation, the Twelfth Knight began some planning and plotting. First, he went to a circus to meet the sword sallower and paid the man to teach him the one trick of that trade. When he was suitably accomplished, he visited a sword maker. He asked him to devise a thin sword with a folding handle. He secretly practiced swallowing the new sword, handle and all, until he was sure that no one could tell what he contained. Of course, he couldn't talk that way, but no son was allowed to address the cruel King at any time.

On the appointed day, as the dozen descendants sat on their stools in the vast Crown Room, number twelve was tight-lipped. He sat in his long knightly napery stiff as a ramrod.

The kind spoke: "I have just received a billet-doux from the really rich Virgin Queen of Prussia, giving her permission to be courted by our Number Twelve Son. Come up here to the front, son, and tell us all about it."

Whoops!

CHAPTER 129 - I FLY

I am a bright yellow Stearman Biplane. Boeing once built thousands of trainers like me (8,584), but not many of us are left. I'd like to live forever and I will if someone keeps me clean, oiled, and inspected. I don't think I will ever crash if I fly alertly and on my best behavior. They say that I am inefficient and old-fashioned, but I think I'm. a lot prettier than all these slick new monoplanes and jets that cost a hundred times more and have no personality. My seven cylinder Continental engine is still strong, and my wings and flippers are covered by the finest first class muslin that by now has several dozen coats of dope and paint.

My cockpit does not concern me, that's just where the pilot sits. He pulls and pushes my stick and rudder and reads some gauges that I don't understand. My pedals don't have brakes, but, hey, who needs them? My tail skid can stop me easily enough. I can take off in 300 feet and land in about the same distance. That's when I like to fly, when the air is hard and cold. My 220 horsepower engine really gulps the air down and puts out. I spend most of my time just sitting at a little airport, in rain, snow, wind, and dust, waiting for the pilot to take me up. These young guys walk around and inspect me like they know what they are doing. So how come they never see that dent in my fuel line, that cracked bolt in my wing, or that jammed pulley in my rear end rudder control? But I try to compensate.

Last week a talented lady pilot came to fly me. I figured she had rented me for an hour or two. After she checked my oil and filled my tank, she started my engine. We were a little stiff and awkward for a half a minute while I blew out white smoke, but then I settled down to a smooth idle of "pocket-t-pocket-t-pocket-f." Someone pulled out the chocks and we began to roll. As we taxied out, we both checked the wind. The runway was empty so she steered me onto it and we sat there at minute, then took a deep breath. Now filled with courage, she pushed the throttle to the firewall. The cool gasoline gushed into my throat as I leapt forward down the strip, straining in every engine mount. We roared and it felt good. I was eager to pull my wheels off the asphalt, but she held me down until 1 was going so fast I leaped into the air all by myself. Then she pulled my nose really high and we zoomed as never before. The cool air and excess gasoline made me tingle in every welded joint. Higher and higher, I couldn't get enough and neither could she. We leveled off to a steady one hundred-mile-an- hour cruise right at cloud level. what a scary thrill as my propeller pulled us deep into a solid white cloud and out the other side into the sun again! Talk about fun, you had to be there.

After a couple of wonderful hours, we circled a city and an airport that I had never seen. A small tower flashed us a green light, so we came in with the half circle approach. We landed solidly, a good three-pointer, but it pained my cracked bolt and stiffened my bad pulley eves more. We taxied up to a welcoming committee who applauded my exhaust pipe's last gasp. She got out of the cockpit and helped put some chocks under my balding tires. The group did a lot of yakking and exchanged some papers, them they all drove off in some dumb automobiles.

Now alone again, I cooled off and relaxed. On the nearest hangar, I saw a curious sign that read, "Welcome To Our New Air Museum."

CHAPTER 130 - SAFARI SO GOOD

He wandered alone, away from the Sitmar Safari Tours camp under the scraggly windblown thorn trees, to get a clear view of the billions of stars in the heavens. A full golden moon frustrated his plan with its brilliance. Nearby, a vertical wall of rock looked like it could provide enough moon shade for star gazing, so he started to saunter in that direction.

It was farther away than he thought, but he was not one to worry. His grandfather had paid for the trip to celebrate his coming of age. He had just walked into total darkness when he stumbled over what seemed like a body. Snarls and yelps made him realize he had bumped into a group of hyenas gnawing on a gamey gazelle. He jumped straight up, then darted away in the darkness. Glowing eyes and glistening fangs followed him as he realized he was being further cut off from the camp.

He vaguely saw a ledge-like lane leading past the corner of the rock wall. It was barely wide enough for his retreat and the edge dropped off into an inky abyss, but he welcomed it.

Now the aggressive carrion eaters could only come at him in a single file, so he could keep kicking the front attacker back as he hobbled along the ever-narrowing ledge on one leg. He was sliding his hands along the surface of the wall, hoping for a handhold, or even a finger hold, when suddenly his hands touched something. There was a blank in the wall.

He reached blindly for something to grab onto, then he brushed against something like fur. A lion's tremendous roar and putrid breath hit him right in the face with a force that stunned his senses. His ears closed, his heart pounded, his breath stopped and he was bathed in an instant cold sweat. He realized he was leaning away from the head, leaning too much, as he was now starting to fall into the night below, with a hyena clamped on his ankle.

He was falling faster and faster, his brain telling him such a long fall would be fatal. His body suddenly slapped hand into water and he was going down like a rock. As his descent slowed, he felt his pant leg being snagged by what only could have been thor branches. He remembered the thorn trees of the camp.

He struggled frantically to free himself even as he realized he did not know which way was up. His lungs screamed for air as his mind began to accept the inevitable. A shocking jerk on his right boot by a set of very sharp teeth pulled him loose from the thorns and up to the surface where he gulped air and water as two crocodiles fought over him.

The croc with the boot in his mouth started rotating violently, throwing him up in the air. He landed on a moonlit riverbank, minus a boot. Dimly, he saw a croc eating a hyena.

After a while, he limped back into the friendly yellow campfire light. The tour guide asked, "Where is your other boot?"

He replied, "A crocodile ate it."

"Sure, sure," said the guide. We'll find it in the morning, now go to bed."

CHAPTER 131 - PATENT IT! GET RICH!

How many times have you seen someone look at a homemade device and exclaim, "Oh, that's clever, you should patent it. You'll be a millionaire."

"They" have been saying that for 200 years. What poverty of mind surfaces here? When my neighbor George made the above acclamation about my new gewgaw, I tried to cure him by asking, "Oh really, do you think I should apply for a Utility Patent, a Design Patent, or just a Trademark or Copyright?" He smiled weakly. I continued, "After I engage a Patent Attorney and his favorite drafting organization, they will start the application for a few thousand, plus a few hundred for a patent search. But how many claims do you think I could win?" George looked for an exit. "Then, after the automatic rejections and revisions, at my expense, if I should be granted a patent in two or three years, what should I do with that piece of paper?"

Defensive now, he said, "Well, a patent is worth a lot of money, isn't it?" I looked amazed and asked, "Does the Patent Office send me money?" He beamed, "No, I think you sell it to a manufacturer and then he pays you a royalty. That's how you get rich."

I asked, "Do you have a particular manufacturer in mind for my invention?" "No, not really."

I observed, "Over the years, I've made up a list of about fifty inventions that I believe are patentable, and I could have spent over $250,000 on patents. I would gladly sell that list for forty bucks if I could find a suck...a buyer. How about you?"

At this point George tried to change the subject with a remark. "What do you think of the new watch my wife's boyfriend gave me?" Nice. He started over, "Why don't you make them yourself, or have them made, then you can sell 'em?" Triumphant grin. I explained, "If an item retails for under ten dollars, the parts and labor should be no more than two dollars, preferably one. Then there's labeling, packaging, shipping, billing, thirty day cash discounts, postage, stationery, letterheads, rubber stamps, business checking accounts, bookkeeping, tax receipts, invoices, ledgers, and office equipment and space. To do a decent advertising job you need good type setting, photography, printing, and a flair for brochure type words, plus order blanks and return type postage-free envelopes."

He persisted, "But you can hire an agency to do all that for you, and still make millions." "True, if you have the money. But suppose I make or have made a garage full of these marvelous gizmos. They will sit there forever unless one knows marketing." He protests, "Why you could sell them to your friends and neighbors, why I might even buy one." "Oh, really? I thought you'd expect one for a gift." He tried, "Out them in the chain stores, they buy carloads." I said, "Chain store buyers are difficult to see and difficult period. If one has a line of several products and a great track record in sales, they may listen, but they try to stay away from home workshop inventors or anyone else with only one item. And what if they say, 'How much for a hundred dozen and can you deliver in thirty days?'" George beams, "Great! Far out, man!" I smiled. "It might be fun to make a dozen or so, but a hundred dozen? I would need more help, space, tools, and reliable suppliers of parts and materials, or find a willing subcontractor to make the whole smear."

He offered, "You could sell them by putting an ad in the paper."

"Yes," I agreed, "I could take out a tiny ad in the Sunday paper for $100 to $400 a week, or in a national magazine for from $1000 to $3000 a month. Then, if I divide that amount plus my patent costs by the net profit available on each, I will know how many thousand's I have to make and ship each month just to break even. Many, many."

"Can't you patent it yourself?"

"Sure, I could learn to file an application without an attorney, make my own drawings and maybe even do my own patent search. Some large cities have a place in the library where you can look up everything ever patented in your gadget's class, sub-class and sub-sub-class. Of course, my idea of the uniqueness of my idea and that of the Patent Examiner may vary widely, and he gets the last word. It can be done and once you get it, you got 'It'. 'It' is a license to sue anyone who tried to steal your idea. Remember, a big company may have a staff of lawyers and will try to prove that they had the idea before the date on my sweat-soaked patent application. Some just steal it and say, `Screw you'."

George says, "I've heard a lot of stories of guys who made it big."

"Yes, these stores are told, retold, and amplified, but it can be done. If I make a better

mousetrap, it can probably be made cheaper in Korea, Taiwan, Singapore, Hong Kong, or Japan. And if I have obtained a patent in those countries, I can fly over there and sue them in their own courts with one of their lawyers. Good luck. It has been done, it will be done again, once in a while."

George tries, "Sell the idea to a good American company."

"Of course, I can just take my little prototype or even a sketch to a company that makes this kind of thing and offer to sell them the whole deal. Usually, before they look at it, they will ask me to sign a standard form that says that they probably thought of it years ago. However, if there are any indecipherable manufacturing secrets involved, they may offer me a down payment of a royalty—but I'd better have my own attorney by my side."

"If you can think of a catchy name, it will sell itself."

"That's right. A clever name or acronym would get me more publicity than a paid ad. If the Hula Hoop had been called the Centerless Grinder or the Boxing Ring, it might not have made it. Devising an acronym is `a crazy rigmarole of naming your machine." (ACRONYM)

George remarks, "You must be a genius to invent such a thing."

"Of course, but how come most patent attorneys get rich while most inventors do not?"

George is firm. "Patent it, you'll get rich!"

CHAPTER 132 - THE PONY TALE

When the big boom hit the Oklahoma oil fields in the 1920's, some of the Indians who had legal title to their lands made a lot of money. Although some were wasteful, one Comanche was frugal with his semi-annual royalty checks.

He was called Hoppy because his mother had been a kidnapped Hopi. He had little experience with the white man's money, but he decided to use all his royalties to buy ponies. By the time his horse heard had reached a thousand head, he realized that his grazing land could support no more. Maybe, he thought, he should spend some of his wealth on some of the white man's magic toys. "I will buy one of those wagons-with-the-horse-cut-off," he said.

He rode into town on his favorite pony, Pale Face, and stoically ignored the many temptations and distractions of the biggest town in the Pan Handle. You could tell it was the County Seat of Cimarron County. The wealth of oil had brought in an influx of carpetbaggers, but also some legitimate business. One such was a Packard Automobile Dealership right on Man Street.

When Hoppy caught sight of a black Packard Touring Sedan with the top down, it was love at first sight. As he turned his pony around and dismounted, he patted the spotted mount for the first time. Perhaps it was an apology for having seduced by the white man's magic machine.

A salesman grimaced at the unkempt customer and muttered to himself, "Another Ute with the loot." Then he inquired, "May I help you?"

Hoppy decided to adopt the white man's custom of omitting all preliminaries and start the trading pow wow at once. He raised his chin, glowered at the man, and demanded, "How many ponies for this sad looking machine?" The salesman tried to hide his sneer behind his hand and turned to walk away. "Sorry, no ponies, we only take money, or gold or silver, or a check that's good."

"Got one thousand ponies, better than money!" Hoppy boasted. The salesman returned to the native son and suggested, "You could go over there to borrow the two thousand dollars required to buy this machine, which is world's best automobile. Then, when you get your next oil royalty check, you can pay back the money. That way you can buy this big black beauty today."

"You train it for me?" "Oh, you mean driving lessons, absolutely, we will teach you. Look, this beauty has two spare tires, and gasoline, oil and water cans mounted on the running board. It can race along at fifty miles in an hour and it has fifty horses under the hood." As he walked across the street to the bank, Hoppy wondered just where the horses were hidden.

The rotund banker was experienced in dealing with the oil-rich natives and found them quite profitable. He greeted Hoppy with a warm bow, then greeted, "How may I help you, Sir?"

Hoppy stayed cool. "Want borrow two thousand dollars, pay you back next royalty check."

The banker smiled politely and asked, "Do you have any collateral?" "What is collateral?" "It's something of value that we can lien on, so to speak, if you cannot repay." "Got one thousand ponies," Hoppy bragged. The banker beamed. "That is good news. I'll have you make an X on a piece of paper, and then you can have your loan. The loan and the Packard purchase were consummated and Hoppy was taught the rudiments of driving and auto maintenance. Cautionsly, he drove the big car homeward, while his disconsolate pony, Pale Face, trotted far behind.

A few weeks later, a cavalry colonel from Fort Riley, Kansas, visited the Oklahoma Pan Handle to buy fresh mounts for his troopers. He was paying much higher prices than expected due to the national prosperity and the concurrent inflation factor. Hoppy sold hundreds and received a check with a lot of zeros. He decided to visit the banker where he could cash the check and pay off his car loan at the same time.

Inside the cool building where a new electric fan was making wind, the banker was happy to see the wealthy aborigine. "It is good to see you again, Mister Hoppy. I hear you sold a lot of horses to the Army." Hoppy pulled out the crumpled check and said, "You cash check, I pay back car loan." As the banker handed him a copy of the paid off mortgage, he warned, "It's dangerous to carry around so much cash. Why don't you deposit it here? It will be safe and you can take some out whenever you need it."

The red man pondered. "You mean Hoppy loan money to you?" "Well, that's a quaint way to put it, but yes, correct." Hoppy lowered his busy eyebrows. "You got collateral?" The banker huffed and puffed. "Well, yes, look at this building, the marble walls, the terrazzo floors, those two big crystal chandeliers, the big steel safe—" "You got ponies?" Hoppy interrupted. The banker put the cash in a brown paper bag so the Indian could take it home.

A few weeks later the Stock Market crashed and the banks closed. Most depositors lost their money.

ABOUT THE AUTHOR

Eddy Hill has a colorful past having traveled all over the world for business as well as pleasure. He was in the USAF, was a pilot, an aerospace scientist, and a writing instructor at a local college.

He received many public speaking awards and is a columnist for Stardusters Magazine for the aerospace industry. He has written screen plays, humorous melodramas, short stories and various magazine articles. Eddy lives in Southern California with his wife, Cozy.

www.ingramcontent.com/pod-product-compliance
Lightning Source LLC
Chambersburg PA
CBHW060237290526
45789CB00001B/81